TABLE OF CONTENTS

Introduction 1

Chapter 1: Introduction to Narcissism 4

Chapter 2: The Internal Nature of a Narcissist 26

Chapter 3: The Narcissist's Abuse 46

Chapter 4: Trauma bonding and co-dependency 67

Chapter 5: The Victims of the Narcissist 80

Chapter 6: Narcissism and Evil 105

Chapter 7: The Spiritual Nature of Narcissistic Abuse 116

Chapter 8: Characteristics of a Narcissist 137

Chapter 9: Stories of Narcissists 158

Chapter 10: Narcissism and Family Dynamics 171

Chapter 11: How To Deal With a Narcissist 183

Chapter 12: How To Empower Yourself Against a Narcissist 196

Chapter 13: Ways to Heal From Narcissistic Abuse 217

Introduction

It's important to define abuse, understand narcissism and validate a victim's feelings. Many victims of any kind of abuse often feel alone, traumatized, confused, hopeless, depressed and feel as if no one understands their situation, their plight, or as if no one has been through what they have.

They feel very isolated from others, and usually don't have many people to turn to. Their victim chose them because they had a dependence on this abuser, or the abuser created a false sense of dependence that doesn't really exist but seems it does. They have developed this false dependence and made it seem more intense or serious than it is. You are not alone, there are hundreds and thousands of people dealing with narcissistic abuse and abuse in many forms.

You are not the only person to encounter a narcissist, and yes- this person is that toxic and abusive and does do the most abhorrent, frightening, shocking things that are unimaginable for any human to be able to commit against someone without a care for what they have done. Yes, they do repeated forms of various abuses towards someone and never hold accountability for any of it. Yes, they often behave like disordered children, or worse because children wouldn't do this kind of evil. Narcissists are not normal creatures. They don't behave or think like normal people, and you are not like them, so thank God for creating you to be the normal, healthy wonderful person you are.

You are blessed for not being like these people and this is the reason they chose you- because you are normal, healthy and unlike them, usually very sane. You probably have the traits of being a genuine, loving, kind person and that's what they seek to steal from you. Your anger, confusion, desire to speak out against this person are perfectly normal and rational. Anyone would feel this way.

They seek to steal your love and destroy it, because they possess no true love within themselves and don't know how to truly love. They have become engulfed with their mental illness and disorder.

They are very mentally ill creatures, and even healing and therapy may not be enough to help them. They are the ones in severe need of help, not you, but they will twist it around and pin It all of you and say something is wrong with you. Nothing is wrong with you- you just need the help and therapy and healing from all the toxic painful abuse they have thrown on you. Your feelings are important and there are many people out there who will validate and understand what you are going through.

Chapter 1

INTRODUCTION TO NARCISSISM

What is a Narcissist?

Narcissism seems to be a huge epidemic in today's society, with many people developing this disorder and possessing the negative traits and performing the twisted actions these mentally inept individuals do. This isn't a disorder that only characterizes the one percent out there. There are a large number of people who have come into contact with or who have had dealings with narcissists in many forms from lovers to bosses to family members. These frightening, malignant disordered people seem to be present everywhere in the population.

If you are reading this book, you will have most likely dealt with a narcissist or come across them in some format in your life or have been a tragic victim of these people. A narcissist is akin to a dangerous predator, and they are not just harmless individuals with a disordered personality or pattern of living thinking or ill treatment towards others. Narcissistic treatment towards others can be extremely dangerous toxic and usually wreaks havoc with someone's life.

If you've survived a dysfunctional relationship or scenario with narcissist, bravo to you- and good for you however many people find themselves still attempting to heal or cope with the aftermath of the abuse that has been done to them, are desperately trying to heal or come to grips with it all, or are still dealing with that person or other narcissists that may be present in their life.

If you're confused about whether the seemingly negative person or abuser present in your life is a narcissist, hopefully you'll gain some insight into what it's like to encounter a narcissist, or the traits they have that make them this specific kind of disordered person. Hopefully you will get the answers you're wanting with regards to whether that individual is a narcissist or not and how to recognize this disorder in other abusers.

What is this person that is considered to be a narcissist? Well, a narcissist is someone who possesses a personality disorder which is a scale of five, on the DSM scale. This person has specific traits which include a grandiose sense of self-importance who has a constant need for admiration and attention, although not every narcissist possesses this specific characteristic or trait and doesn't always have a constant need for attention, but still has many of the qualities and characteristics that narcissists generally tend to possess.

Narcissists possess the disorder of narcissism, or narcissistic personality disorder which is typically characterized by a number of unfavorable traits that revolve around the person having a grandiose sense of self-importance, coupled with very low self-esteem. You typically don't want to cross paths with a narcissist, especially if you're a kind, caring individual or someone who possesses traits of being empathic or good in nature. There are varying kinds of narcissists out there which can be placed in several different categories, and all of them are toxic in nature and a kind of person and personality you don't want anything to do with usually, if you are not a narcissist.

A narcissist is a person who has an inflated sense of self-importance, a deep need for admiration and attention, and a lack of empathy for others. They often have an excessive sense of entitlement, and believe they are superior to others. Narcissists may take advantage of others to achieve their own goals, and may become angry or defensive if they feel their sense of self-worth is threatened. Narcissistic personality disorder is a mental health condition characterized by this pattern of behavior.

Narcissistic personality disorder is a mental health condition in which a person has an inflated sense of self-importance, a constant need for admiration and attention, and a lack of empathy for others. People with NPD may have grandiose ideas about their own abilities and achievements, and may exaggerate their accomplishments or talents. They may also be preoccupied with fantasies of power, success, and attractiveness.

To be diagnosed with NPD, a person must exhibit a persistent pattern of these behaviors, and the behavior must cause significant distress or impairment in their life, such as difficulties with relationships or work. Treatment for NPD typically involves talk therapy, and medication may be prescribed to treat co-occurring conditions such as depression or anxiety.

Some traits that someone with narcissistic personality disorder possess are as follows:

Grandiose sense of self-importance.

Narcissists possess a unique and false sense of self importance and feel they are above others. This is the belief that your presence and work is essential to the happiness or success of other people and any enterprises or relationships.

Exaggerated sense of self-importance.

Feeling superior to others and that one deserves special treatment. Feelings are often accompanied by fantasies of unlimited success, brilliance, power, beauty, or love

Preoccupation with fantasies of unlimited success, power, brilliance, beauty or ideal love.

This describes the idea or belief that you are capable of exceptionally high levels of achievement even when your skills or abilities show evidence that is contrary. Belief that he or she is special and unique and can only be understood by, or should associate with, other special or high-status people or institutions.

Need for excessive admiration.

They demand that others admire their appearance, accomplishments, skills, or existence. The admiration of others is what feeds the narcissist. Boasting is second nature to narcissists, and compliments are believed to be proof of their superiority. Must be the center of attention. Often monopolizes conversations, Often feels slighted, mistreated, depleted, and enraged when ignored.

Interpersonally exploitive behavior.

Narcissists see other people as tools. Others exist solely as objects for the narcissist to use and abuse at their own whim or pleasure. They lack self-awareness and the idea that others have their own feelings or beliefs. Whatever they ask for, it's in their own interest and they have no guilt for this.

Lack of empathy.

They lack empathy and do not care about how others feel or might think about something. They only tend to care about their own feelings or perceptions, and the outcome of scenarios and interactions with others. Severely limited or lacking the ability to care about the emotional needs or experiences of others, even loved ones

Envy of others or belief that others are envious of him or her.

This describes the narcissist's constant comparison of themselves to others, wishing for themselves the success others experience, and the false belief that everyone else is envious of them. That's how they keep their egos intact. They cannot handle having a normal ego or perceiving themselves like everyone else. This behavior or thinking usually stems from delusional beliefs they may possess.

Arrogant behaviors or attitudes.

They often have traits of arrogance and conceit and tend to disrespect the rights of others and expect others to bend to their will or demands. They often possess exploitative behavior and use it as they please, and feel they have the right to do what they want to others without consequences or care.

Not every narcissist possesses every trait listed, however most do have traits of being habitual liars, take advantage of others, have a false sense of self, have an outer self and inner self which they tend to keep separate, and never take responsibility for any actions or mistakes they have committed.

The origins of Narcissism:

Narcissism has a long history, going back to ancient Greece but made famous by a Roman poet. The earliest reference to Narcissus in Western literature is a mention of the Narcissus flower. The Greek poet Homer tells us that it was the seductive charm of the narcissus flower which tempted the young girl Persephone and thrust her into hell.

In the first century, the Roman poet Ovid created a poem "The Metamorphoses," in which Narcissus was involved in an ill-fated love story. In Ovid's tale, Narcissus is a much-pursued handsome adolescent boy who, because of his "cold pride," does not return the love of anyone who wants to get close to him. Narcissus's parents were the God of the River, Cephissus, and the nymph Liriope.

Narcissus was told by a therapist that he would live a long life if he did not come to know himself. Narcissus had rejected many lovers by this time, and one had prayed to the goddess nemesis for revenge. He asks Nemesis, that Narcissus fall in love but never possess the object of his love. Narcissus is then lead to the pool of water where he falls in love with his own godlike image.

He was unable to remove himself from looking at his own reflection but soon realized that his love could not be reciprocated when he attempted to kiss or hold the reflection. However, his confusion is amplified when the image in the pool reciprocated his winks and waves. Narcissus could not understand why he could not secure what he so desperately desired. Narcissus was tormented by this and by the time he realized it was his reflection it was too late, and he had already fallen in love with himself. Because he now knew he could never obtain what he truly wanted his body melted away from the passion he felt burning inside him.

When a nymph who Narcissus rejected, Echo, returns to the place where Narcissus had been staring into his own eyes to recover his body for the funeral, she found in his place a gold and white flower. This flower would become known as the Narcissus flower, or the daffodil. Looking at his image in water, Narcissus pines away from unrequited love, and had metamorphosized into a white flower.

What is a personality disorder

A personality disorder is a type of mental disorder in which you have a rigid and unhealthy pattern of thinking, functioning and behaving. A person with a personality disorder has trouble perceiving and relating to situations and people. This causes significant problems and limitations in relationships, social activities, work and school.

In some cases, you may not realize that you have a personality disorder because your way of thinking and behaving seems natural to you. And you may blame others for the challenges you face.

Personality disorders usually begin in the teenage years or early adulthood. There are many types of personality disorders. Some types may become less obvious throughout middle age.

A personality disorder is a long-standing pattern of behavior, thinking, and functioning that deviates significantly from cultural norms and expectations. This pattern of behavior usually manifests in adolescence or early adulthood, and often persists throughout the person's life. Personality disorders are typically characterized by a persistent and inflexible pattern of behavior that causes significant distress or impairment in social, occupational, or other areas of functioning.

There are several different types of personality disorders, each with its own set of specific symptoms and patterns of behavior. Some common features of personality disorders may include extreme rigidity in thought and behavior, difficulty in forming and maintaining close relationships, and a tendency towards emotional instability or impulsivity.

It's important to note that having a personality disorder doesn't necessarily mean that a person is flawed or morally deficient. Many people with personality disorders can lead successful and fulfilling lives with the right treatment and support. Effective treatment for personality disorders may include therapy, medications, and self-help strategies to help people manage their symptoms and improve their overall quality of life.

How to diagnose someone with narcissistic personality disorder

There are various kinds of narcissism out there that can be defined within this spectrum, however those who have these traits of narcissism which include a lack of empathy for others, a desire for attention and praise, and a sense of entitlement, may not be diagnosed with NPD. In order to be diagnosed with Narcissistic personality disorder, Mental health providers will use the Diagnostic and Statistical Manual, to clinically diagnose someone with NPD. A diagnosis requires a qualified mental health professional to assess the person for personality dysfunction among multiple domains and the expression of specific personality traits.

NPD is a mental health disorder that leads to significant distress or impairment in social, occupational, or other important areas of functioning in a person's life. A person has to fit criteria for this disorder in order to receive a diagnosis. Some experts believe there are five types of narcissism, while others feel there are nine or 10.

The Diagnostic and Statistical Manual of Mental Disorders (DSM) is the handbook widely used by clinicians and psychiatrists in the United States to diagnose psychiatric illnesses. The DSM covers all categories of mental health disorders for both adults and children.

It contains descriptions, symptoms, and other criteria necessary for diagnosing mental health disorders. It also contains statistics concerning who is most affected by different types of illnesses, the typical age of onset, the development and course of the disorders, risks and prognostic factors, and other related diagnostic issues.

In addition to other specified criteria, the DSM-5 narcissism guidelines also point out nine different features of narcissistic personality disorder that professionals recognize

1. Inflated self-esteem or a grandiose sense of self-importance or superiority
2. Craving admiration
3. Exploitative relationships (i.e., manipulation)
4. Little to no empathy
5. Identity is easily disturbed (i.e., can't handle criticism)
6. Lack of attachment and intimacy
7. Feelings of depression or emptiness when not validated
8. A sense of entitlement
9. Can feel like others are envious of them, or may envy others

An individual must have at least five out of nine of these traits, many of which can start appearing at a young age.

Some clinicians believe that there are 10 different kinds of narcissists that exist

- Classic narcissists, who have a grandiose sense of self and entitlement.
- Vulnerable narcissists, who have low self-esteem and seek validation from others.

- Communal narcissists, who exploit their involvement in altruistic causes for their own benefit.
- Malignant narcissists, who have antisocial, sadistic, and paranoid traits.
- Somatic narcissists, who are obsessed with their physical appearance and attractiveness.
- Cerebral narcissists, who flaunt their intelligence and achievements.
- Inverted narcissists, who are codependent on other narcissists.
- Overt narcissists, who are openly arrogant and manipulative.
- Covert narcissists, who are secretly resentful and envious of others.
- Hypervigilant narcissists, who are constantly on guard for threats and criticism.
- Grandiose narcissists, who have an inflated sense of superiority and dominance.
- Exhibitionist narcissists, who crave attention and admiration from others.
- Sexual narcissists, who use sex as a way to exploit and control others.
- Vindictive narcissists, who seek revenge and harm on those who oppose or reject them.

The narcissist has a multi-faceted disorder

Most narcissists who are also categorized as abusers towards the victims they choose, can be put into several of these categories or do exhibit traits from varying categories listed, not necessarily just one. Narcissists generally don't possess traits from simply just one of these categories, as most have a number of issues and problems and combined can be placed in several different categories. Many narcissists who might be considered malignant and have sadistic traits, might also be classic narcissists, and also have a sense of low self esteem as well, and tend to hide that notion about them and inflate it with a grandiose sense of self.

Many narcissists unfortunately possess traits of psychopathy and sociopathy as well and are not decent people to know or to come across, though they throw out their false sense of self one which they show to the world and to others as being perfect, incapable of evil or wrongdoing, and one which they project outward to others and perfect in order to show everyone they are good and decent human beings. Narcissists are anything but perfect, good, decent noble people who are incapable of harm or wrongdoing- they are the people who do the most harm and wrong especially to their victims and are one of the most dangerous creations out there.

Narcissists simply don't want to look within themselves and perceive their true flaws, or figure out what is truly going on inside of them or what is wrong with them. They lack any concept of introspection and want to believe they are a flawless perfect individual incapable of doing no harm or wrong to anyone, and that they are like any normal person out there.

Ironically, they are in fact some of the most destructive and damaging individuals out there and this lack of introspection will only add to the toxic environment they create for themselves and those around them who end up being victims of theirs. The rest of the world and society will never get to see the true and real narcissist, the pathology that lies within, or experience the hidden abuse they force upon those unfortunate people who end up being the sole victims of the narcissist.

The Narcissist is by far the most flawed human to exist, and one of the few humans, like most abusers out there that fail to recognize, care for or admit the flaws present that exist within this extremely disordered, and dangerous creature that seems to comprise an unhealthy number out there today when it comes to personality types and disorders.

The different types of narcissists
Covert Narcissist:

A covert narcissist is a type of narcissistic personality disorder in which a person displays many of the traits of traditional narcissism, but in a more subtle or "hidden" way. While traditional or overt narcissists may exhibit grandiose behavior and demand attention and admiration from others, covert narcissists tend to be more reserved and self-effacing, often presenting as modest or even self-deprecating.

Despite their outward appearance of humility or shyness, covert narcissists are still focused on themselves and can be highly manipulative and emotionally abusive to those around them. They may use passive-aggressive tactics to maintain control in their relationships, such as guilt-tripping, playing the victim, or using subtle forms of criticism or judgment to undermine others.

Some of the key characteristics of covert narcissism might include a lack of empathy, a preoccupation with their own feelings and needs, a tendency to manipulate others for personal gain, and difficulty accepting criticism or feedback from others. Because the signs of covert narcissism may be less obvious than those of overt narcissism, it can be more challenging to identify and address, particularly for those who are in close relationships with individuals who exhibit these traits.

Overt Narcissist:

An overt narcissist is a type of narcissistic personality disorder (NPD) in which a person displays many of the classic traits of narcissism in a more outwardly obvious and attention-seeking way. Overt narcissists tend to have an inflated sense of self-importance and seek constant admiration and attention from others. They may put on a facade of charm or charisma to manipulate those around them into fulfilling their desires and demands.

Some of the key characteristics of overt narcissism might include a lack of empathy, a preoccupation with their own feelings and needs, a sense of entitlement, a tendency to manipulate others for personal gain, and a willingness to exploit or take advantage of others.

Overt narcissists may also display grandiose behavior, such as boasting, exaggerating their accomplishments or contributions, or seeking out positions of power and authority. They may become angry or defensive when confronted with criticism or feedback that challenges their self-image, and may respond with gaslighting or other forms of emotional manipulation to maintain their apparent superiority.

While overt narcissists can often be highly successful and charismatic in their social and professional lives, their relationships can be fraught with conflict, exploitation, and emotional abuse. It is important to seek professional help if you or someone you know is exhibiting symptoms of overt narcissism, in order to address the underlying emotional and psychological issues that can contribute to these problematic behaviors.

Malignant narcissist:

A malignant narcissist is a particularly dangerous and destructive form of narcissistic personality disorder (NPD) that involves a combination of narcissistic traits and antisocial or sociopathic behaviors. People with malignant narcissism are characterized by an intense and pervasive sense of grandiosity and entitlement, along with a callous disregard for the feelings and well-being of others.

Some of the key characteristics of malignant narcissism might include extreme narcissistic behavior, a lack of empathy, a willingness to exploit or manipulate others for personal gain, a tendency towards sadism or cruelty, and a lack of concern for social or moral norms.

Malignant narcissists may be highly skilled at manipulating others, often using a combination of charm, flattery, and aggressive or abusive behavior to control and dominate those around them. They may be prone to explosive outbursts of anger or rage, and may become violent or vindictive when they feel their sense of superiority or power is threatened.

Because of their extreme lack of empathy and their willingness to exploit and hurt others, malignant narcissists pose a significant danger to those around them. If you suspect that you or someone you know may be exhibiting signs of malignant narcissism, it is important to seek professional help in order to address the underlying emotional and psychological issues that may be driving these behaviors, and to protect yourself and others from potential harm.

There are different ways to categorize narcissism depending on the approach, but three common types of narcissism are:

1. Grandiose narcissism: characterized by a need for admiration, sense of superiority, and often an inflated sense of self-importance. People with grandiose narcissism may come across as charming or charismatic, but deep down have a fragile self-esteem that is propped up by the opinions of others.
2. Vulnerable narcissism: characterized by a fragile self-esteem, hypersensitivity to criticism or rejection, and a tendency to feel victimized by others. People with vulnerable narcissism may struggle with feelings of shame, self-doubt, and low self-esteem, which can lead to defensive or hostile behavior towards others.
3. Malignant narcissism: as mentioned previously, it is a subtype of narcissism that combines grandiose narcissistic traits with antisocial, psychopathic, or sadistic behavior. People with

malignant narcissism show little regard for others' feelings or rights, and their behaviors often have harmful or destructive outcomes.

It's important to note that narcissism is a complex and multifaceted personality disorder, and individuals can exhibit different combinations of these traits and behaviors. Additionally, not all people with narcissistic traits meet the criteria for a diagnosis of narcissistic personality disorder, and not everyone with narcissistic personality disorder exhibits abusive or harmful behavior towards others.

Narcissism, sociopathy and psychopathy

What is a sociopath psychopath or narcissist and what are the key differences when it comes to these traits versus narcissism? Both psychopathy and sociopathy are characterized by a pattern of disregard for and violation of the rights of others. Lack of guilt, remorse, and a disregard for other people's rights also are traits that are present in people with these disorders.

A sociopath is a person with a personality disorder that is marked by traits of impulsivity, risk-taking, and violence. A psychopath is a person who has an antisocial personality disorder characterized by a lack of regard for the rights and feelings of others, controlled and manipulative behaviors, the absence of shame, and an inability to form emotional relationships. Deceit and manipulation are central aspects of both personality types. However, even though they are often confused with one another because they manifest in similar ways, these are two distinct forms of personality disorders.

Both psychopathy and sociopathy, share features with narcissistic personality disorder. Like persons with these other disorders, narcissists generally lack empathy and tend to have unrealistically high opinions of themselves, and, like psychopaths, narcissists tend to form shallow relationships, to exploit and manipulate others, and to be glib and superficially charming.

A psychopath is a person who exhibits a persistent pattern of antisocial behaviors, such as lying, manipulation, impulsivity, and a lack of regard for the rights and feelings of others. Psychopaths may be charming and appear normal on the surface, but they typically lack the ability to feel empathy or remorse for their actions and may have a reckless disregard for the safety or well-being of others.

Psychopathy is not an official diagnosis in the Diagnostic and Statistical Manual of Mental Disorders (DSM-5), but it is often associated with the diagnosis of antisocial personality disorder. While not all people with antisocial personality disorder are psychopaths, research has shown that psychopaths are more likely to exhibit severe and persistent antisocial behavior, and may pose a greater risk to society than those with other forms of antisocial personality disorder.

A sociopath is a person who exhibits a persistent pattern of antisocial behaviors, such as lying, manipulation, impulsivity, and a lack of regard for the rights and feelings of others. Sociopaths may be charming and appear normal on the surface, but they typically lack the ability to feel empathy or remorse for their actions and may have a reckless disregard for the safety or well-being of others.

The term "sociopath" is often used interchangeably with the term "psychopath," and there is some overlap between the two terms. However, some experts use the term "sociopath" to describe a person who is more impulsive and erratic in their behavior, while "psychopath" is used to describe someone who is more calculating and

Chapter 2

The Internal Nature of a Narcissist

Narcissists lack a conscience

The Narcissist is a glib, shallow, fake shell of a person who is severely disordered with a host of issues and problems. They often exploit others to get what they want, and do much worse . Good luck trying to reason or argue with a narcissist, or anyone that has this disorder or these traits. This is because they are incapable of arguing when the argument has to do with their self-inflection inwards, or regarding any mistakes they have made or character flaws they may possess. That is because, the narcissist is incapable of admitting their mistakes or feel that they're incapable of making mistakes.

Now, when they put on their grandiose or false sense of self that they present to the world, they might be able to fake a ploy and fake admit any mistakes they have done or pretend they are admitting to them in order to appear like a normal person to others, though even that being done is far fetched when dealing with a narcissist. The narcissist will often put on a façade of who they really are to others.

They will appear caring, kind, doting, genuine, empathetic while deep down possessing extreme bitterness and self-loathing within. Narcissists refuse to look inward at the mess that is their true self, or the mess that is their true personality and morals within, and any accusation you point at them is not only a threat to their false sense of self or fake ego they've created in order to convince themselves they're normal, healthy, happy normal people, but it's a threat to their very core and lack of soul and realizing their soul is extremely damaged, and a way for them to have to look inwards which is something they are incapable of doing due to the damage it would do to their own self and sense of self.

If they have to look within their very souls and admit to the evils they have already done to their unfortunate victims, or to what they truly possess inside and who they really are, they would be unable to handle this frightening, complex mess. They refuse to do this very basic thing, because they are incapable of handling the real fragile distorted, damaged sense of self that the narcissist truly possesses, also the fact that they lack a working conscience or a real and true intelligent mind.

They also lack the proper state of mind and conscience to be able to handle the very evils they have committed or they are capable of committing, who their very essence is, and the fact that their very lack of conscience is incapable of handling this complex frightening mess that is the narcissists's very soul and ego, or what has become of them now.

Most narcissists were usually always characterized by this disorder in some form at a younger age, but their narcissistic tendencies may not have been as prevalent in early age, yet tend to get worse as they get older, or even due to external circumstances which may occur and trigger this downward spiral in their selves and core selves. For example, they may have encountered or even been abused by other narcissists or abusers, which in turn they were unable to handle, which brought forth their own narcissism and it may have slowly developed unknowing to them over time.

Narcissists lack any form of introspection

They lack any form of introspection or self-awareness and have created such a complex dysfunction within their very mind it is impossible for their ego, mind, conscience and soul to grasp any of it and they mask it with extreme and intense projections onto others, minimizing their wrong or evil behaviors or actions, denying, and blaming others for this. They have created a very dysfunctional false sense of self and this false sense of self is a very complicated puzzle of nonsense and sickness that they use to project to the world, to others and to themselves that they are normal, decent and perfect apart from evil or wrong.

This false sense of self is cradling their very fragile ego and true sense of self, a mess of anger, self-loathing, bitterness and hatred that has developed for decades that is a very fragile, crumbled nothingness of an ego, which is the narcissist's real and true self- the self they project so mercilessly onto their victims, and their very core, which is dark and lacking of empathy and devoid of any true happiness or good. It's impossible to argue with a narcissist or attempt to pinpoint anything you feel they may have done that is perceived as a wrong to you, or even a mistake they made, because they will go all out and perceive this as a huge threat to the fake or false sense of self they have created, which is comprised of delusional beliefs, lack of awareness or introspection, compressing, minimizing and denying the evil creation they are, and the blaming they have done to others for their very own actions upon them, or towards others.

Narcissists never take responsibility for their actions

Attempting to blame them for any of their actions, will trigger the disordered narcissist to lash out at you for threatening their very sense of self, attempting to shatter their false sense of self which they have taken many years to perfect and which is already a mess since it is fake and not who they truly are or how they really feel inside about anything. It will force them to turn into the angry, loathing monster they really are inside, threaten that portion of them to take over them, which they in turn can't handle about their lives, which they tend to find empty and meaningless deep down and make them fear that their fragile ego and meaningless true sense of self they possess will take over, rather than the false sense of self they'd rather have present.

They refuse to believe they've committed any wrongdoing or have harmed their victims' lives in any form. They will fight this idea to the bitter end, and tend to lash out even more at anyone who threatens their sense of self and their lack of morals-whether it's their victims or anyone attacking their character or persona in any way. They will tend to blame the victims if it's someone else doing this, and if it's the victims they will deny any wrongdoing to the person, and project, minimize, deny and blame the victim and even abuse, gaslight, or attack them further and do even more damage to them often times in a sadistic nature.

Narcissists are full of bitterness, rage, hatred, and hostile emotions and feelings and use their victims to project their inner turmoil out on because they can't handle possessing these emotions or feelings and have no knowledge of how to process them.

The internal makeup of a narcissist

The narcissist has an inability to deal with life traumas, issues, disappointments and major events that might happen in a human's life. They have an immature way of processing life's problems and a lack of cognitive development in their inner mind and being something that took place at a young age for them.

They lack the concept of being able to process trauma, normal occurrences in life, and life's lessons in a healthy normal way and do so through extreme suppression, inner anger, rage, deep-rooted hated self-loathing, and lack of self-introspection or awareness of their own feelings or beliefs. They will then begin to harness feelings which they've repressed for years which were never dealt with or processed, and begin to choose targets and rage and lash out at them for being unable to handle any kind of problem in life, and begin to blame the victim or targets for this and believe their delusional ideas and irrational thoughts.

The narcissists often live in a fantasy world. They believe they are the center of it all and that they have been the ones victimized not the victims. They soothe and cater to these false lies and delusions that they live by. They live in a world of hatred and self-loathing. They enjoy creating hostility and a dysfunctional family dynamic and will breed and create other narcissists through their collective behaviors and actions. They may even abuse golden children or others in order to employ their covert abusive tactics and traumatize that person so that their development is flawed or that their happiness or growth is stunted.

Most narcissists are full of anger, hate, self-loathing, hate and rage within. They are angry at their lives and others and lack many forms of empathy, and have turned into vicious hateful disordered predators.

Narcissists are delusional

Narcissists are very delusional. They will rage on a victim, do horrible things to people and then twist and turn it all around and claim that the victim committed these very deeds and actions, and that they did nothing to the victim, nothing wrong to the victim, or use tactics to convince others the victim deserved the things that they did to them-they did it for their own good in some way. Narcissists will never hold accountability for their actions and will always blame a victim.

They may sometimes apologize to a victim depending on the situation, if asked, but they are never remorseful, for they don't believe, or want to believe they've done anything wrong, and they are so mentally ill, they've convinced themselves for years that the victim is the problem and is doing everything wrong and is the cause for the problem and have gotten used to blaming the victim for their own sick evil behaviors towards them.

They will convince others of these delusional and irrational thoughts and behaviors. They will even often convince their targets of being delusional or having irrational thoughts- anything that the narcissist possesses within themselves, they will throw out onto the victims.

Narcissists hate themselves

Narcissists hate themselves and their true selves within, yet they project an ideation and image of being perfect and normal people, even great or moral people. they usually denigrate and abuse and choose objects to degrade and ruin, and will further punish those objects for even being close to them in some form, and for a perceived neediness they feel that person has towards them. They will often punish victims harshly and in their own cruel sadistic ways.

The narcissist will often accuse the victim of being what they are. They will resort to extreme accusations, insults and detailed descriptions of very strange concepts including describing their own victims as narcissists if they ever have a chance to or the knowledge.

This is a frightening concept known as projection. Most narcissists do not have any detailed knowledge of narcissism or have heard of or know about the disorder. There are some that do, but most live in a state of complete oblivion to something like this. They believe they are emblems of moral perfection, decency and goodness and have wronged no one.

Anyone who makes any just accusation towards them will be punished for being delusional, crazy, and accused of being the abuser. Any victim is usually horrified at the characteristics the narcissist keeps throwing upon them, especially once they realize these things are in fact exactly what the narcissist are or actions they are secretly doing. They seem to be unaware of the projections they are unleashing upon someone, and it's part of their frightening disorder and illness.

Many times, the narcissist will secretly and unknowingly tell you disturbing things about themselves by projecting. You will be spewed with this toxic venom of harrowing qualities many of which are too disturbing to be able to respond to. I once had dealt with a narcissist, who was constantly projecting at me and was telling me all the horrible detailed things he was doing secretly, by accusing me of those things.

Narcissists aren't oblivious to their negative interactions with people though they will often staunchly deny behaving this way or being negative at all. This is to discredit the distraught confused victim, invalidate their feelings, never give them their power back, and to continue the cycle of hostility towards them.

Narcissists are full of dark energy

Narcissists have developed into natural energy vampires and carry a natural darkness within them, something that has developed within them their own lives. They are wrought with negative and dark energies that are full of a host of very toxic emotions and thoughts and experiences that have been suppressed by them. You'll often find that narcissists rarely vent to family or friends in their life about their problems and if they do, it doesn't solve their issues or gives them a way to be able to mentally cope with or deal with those issues, so they will resort to the misery that makes up the narcissist-just turn into a battery of charged unresolved emotions that are usually dark in nature.

The narcissist will often steal your power energy or soul in major ways in order to create a codependent relationship with you, create fierce trauma bonds, leave you stripped of your very soul and inner life force feeling empty and dead inside and in need of it back, with the hopes that you will be so weak traumatized brittle and unable to cope with or move on or feel powerful strong or independent so you can forever stay in the grips of this monster and they can further victimize you.

They will solidify the trauma bonds by love bombing you and being nice to you and acting normal so that you'll forgive them and be glad they are behaving normally finally so they can condition you into this repetitive dark pattern they've created, and so you can never regain your power or break free of them.

They will attack you at whim and begin this terrifying cycle of abuse when you least expect it and because their abuse is so harsh and damaging full of so many elements, you will be unable to handle or process it at all and then begins their devaluation phase designed to destroy you and allow them to steal your power or energy, soul and more feel powerful and vindicated, yet they will never truly feel better or vindicated. Inside, They are still the negative diseased monsters they have always been, and you the destroyed victim.

The trauma bonds are often full of the narcissist's dark energy and your own positive good energy and the dysfunctional madness they have created between you and they but more so true narcissist stealing your power and energy.

They will possess your energy and soul to a great extent, and you will be very drained, depleted and in need of them to regain your power back and worse off for any kind of positive energy or support.

Even if they are nice once again and you don't really need them to regain your energy back, you will still feel a need for them because they have created a dysfunctional codependency between the two of you and you feel you need them for a variety of reasons.

Narcissists hate being criticized

Narcissists typically don't respond well to being criticized, analyzed, labeled, or having theories placed about them because they believe themselves to be perfect, having no flaws, and even if they know they do have flaws, which deep down they simply do not believe, they will never admit to their flaws, attitudes, issues, and shortcomings unless it's in a way that is boosting their sense of self, their false self that they project outwards to others, or unless they made a mistake and showed some character flaw of theirs and need to apologize or otherwise maintain themselves to appear to be perfect and genuine, decent human beings.

Most people in general don't enjoy being criticized or labeled either, but it's different with a narcissist- a narcissist is generally a heavily toxic and dangerous person and creation that can do substantial damage to a person or victim and it's necessary to understand and label them for what they are, rather than trying to ignore this very dangerous personality disorder that does incorporate the traits of psychopathy and sociopathy. According to the DSM-IV there are three main types of narcissism and several different sub-types of this disorder.

Narcissists have a number of traits internally that you may not think they would have, feelings, thoughts and ideas that they will hide deep down or keep secret from others. The abuse narcissist's do to others can sink deep and can be a horrible thing to experience. While, it is usually not a one-time experience or thing, the nature of the attack they do to others can hold deep-rooted negativity for the victim.

Narcissistic Vulnerability

Narcissists may seem to have strong personalities, but deep down they are actually vulnerable. Some therapists feel they are fragile. They suffer from emptiness, alienation, powerlessness and often times feel their life lacks meaning. Due to their fear of losing control, and lack of self-esteem, they crave power and will try to control their environment, people around them, and their feelings. They are extremely insecure as well.

Narcissistic Shame

Underneath their façade is a lot of shame. Shame makes narcissists feel insecure and inadequate——vulnerable feelings that they must deny to themselves and others. This is one reason that they can't take criticism, responsibility, or negative feedback from others. They resort to anger and hostility over these feelings.

Arrogance

To compensate for feeling inferior, they maintain an attitude of superiority and arrogance. They're often critical, and judgmental and do not approve of other certain people. They are often bullies and put people down or hurt them to make themselves feel better.

Entitlement

Narcissists feel entitled to get what they want from others regardless of their behavior. They convince themselves that they're superior and that they deserve special treatment in some way. They feel they should get free tickets, get in line in front of others, and a list of things. Other people are considered inferior and not separate from them in their disordered mind. They don't recognize their behavior as hypocritical or wrong, because they feel superior and special. Rules don't apply to them.

Lack of Empathy

Narcissists lack empathy. Their ability to respond emotionally and and have concern for others doesn't exist or is severely impaired. They're "unwilling to recognize or identify with the feelings and needs of others." Research shows that they have structural abnormalities in brain regions associated with emotional feelings. They may claim they love you, but you must determine what is really going on based on how they treat you. Real love requires empathy, and compassion. You won't experience this with this them, mostly abuse. Narcissists can be selfish, hurtful, and cold. To them relationships are a way to use others to get their needs met.

Emptiness

Narcissists lack a positive, emotional connection to themselves, making it difficult for them to emotionally connect with others. They have an undeveloped self and deficient inner resources, which causes them to be dependent on others for validation. Rather than having confidence, they actually fear that they're undesirable.

They can only admire themselves based on other people's perception of them. Despite their boasting and self-flattery, they crave attention and constant admiration. They try usually try to control what others think to feel better about themselves. They use relationships for narcissistic supply and to gain confidence.

However, due to their inner emptiness, they're never satisfied. Whatever you do for them is never enough to fill their emptiness. Narcissists exploit and drain others around them.

Lack of Boundaries

Narcissists' inner emptiness, shame, lack of introspection, and an undeveloped mind, make them uncertain of their boundaries. They don't experience other people as separate individuals, but as extensions of themselves, without feelings, since narcissists cannot empathize with others. To them, other people usually exist to meet their needs. Narcissists are selfish and do not care about their impact on others which is why they behave in cruel ways.

Narcissists often have a deep-seated fear of abandonment and rejection. They may hate themselves for feeling dependent on others for validation so they will take their anger out on their victims for having these emotions, which they don't even fully understand or have analyzed.

The false sense of self defined

The narcissist possesses a false sense of self. This false self has been developed and created by the narcissist as a mask solely for the narcissist to be able to survive the internal madness that is their makeup. The false self is the self that the narcissist portrays to the world, which usually is happy, bubbly, normal, healthy, while portraying a very normal person that is like a mask of their true self, which is hidden underneath.

The false self that the narcissist has created has done so automatically, and through other means only because the narcissist uses this self to portray a normal, healthy, person as opposed to all the conflicting feelings, thoughts and emotions that are present within the narcissist's mind, body and soul. The false sense of self is the seemingly perfect self they display to others and the world to prove they are a healthy normal functioning person and not the disordered creature they really are.

Sometimes, the false sense of self they have created was in fact the real narcissist at some point- maybe they were a healthy, caring loving kind individual at some point or somewhat normal, but as their disorder developed, so did other parts to them. That is because most narcissists were created in some form due to dysfunctional abuse that was done to them- whether it was a lack of development in childhood while being abused, or something that happened later in life.

Most of the time, the narcissistic nature of this person developed early on in life, though it may have been exacerbated or worsened by even encountering other abusers or narcissists, and they were just unable to cope with the situation and their dysfunction got worse. Some narcissists may be this way due to genetic reasons and have psychopathic and sociopathic tendencies, however, it's difficult to diagnose and know how many narcissists were made this way or how many were born with this disorder.

The true self of a narcissist

The true self of the narcissist is a study in pathological nature. The narcissist's true self is riddled with a host of negative emotions, traumas, repressed emotions, and a disordered person inside, who is self-loathing and very bitter and a part of them they hide to the world and others. Due to their lack of introspection and wicked natures they fail to and are unable to process other forms of abuse or trauma effectively, or in any form usually resulting in more disorder, repression emotions on their part, and the worsening of their mental illness.

Most of them refuse to get therapy or admit anything is wrong with them, and if they attempted to heal might be unable to handle the idea of all the evils things they have done. Rather than admit to their faults, they just pin the blame onto others, usually their victims. They might crumble or shatter at the very notion of healing and be unable to cope. Many narcissists live in a constant state of anger, fear, confusion, lack of awareness and bitterness. Their true self is usually a shattered, crumbled mess of hatred, negativity and darkness that they try to hide from others.

The narcissist is generally known to have a dual-self present

The narcissist may even have multiple personalities present within their psyche- this is because they are harboring such a disordered personality, that the true creature within really doesn't exist. The narcissists's true self is a collage of rejected negative emotions, thoughts and feelings that the narcissist has suppressed within, ignored, forgotten about and pretended to not exist, not a solid genuine person with a defined personality. This is a person with a personality disorder, and this particular disorder is comprised of extremely chaotic forces, feelings, and thoughts rather than a cohesive, coherent person with a defined thought process and behavior pattern.

The narcissist doesn't think or behave like the average normal person might. Multiple personalities were somehow created due to the narcissist creating not just a dual self or a single Jekyll/Hyde personality, but a number of personalities created due to extreme trauma, and the disorder present there. The narcissist will usually have created various personalities that arise from extreme amounts of trauma, neglect, suppression, and just a part of the disorder. Many will have created a vast number of false selves in order to further cope with having this disorder and lacking the ability to handle it or any normal function or process that takes place within a normal person's mind.

These strange personalities are displayed to people in different forms, and at various times, depending on which person the narcissist wants to be. They might want to be the arrogant, haughty jerk, or they might want to be the jokester with the funny personality out of the blue. Many narcissists don't just harbor a dual self- they have cultivated many different personas and personalities that have been created due to the nature of their disorder at time even automatically, as some sort of frightening mechanism that the disordered narcissist has used to cope with dealing with life in some way, their own trauma, and other events that they have undergone in life.

Chapter 3

The Narcissist's Abuse

*T**he narcissist is often a frightening disordered rage-infested parasite that is extremely dangerous to anyone out there, especially it's prey, and that does the ultimate forms of damage to its victims. You can compare this person to a shark, or an alligator in nature, a natural predator yet those creatures don't possess an abnormality or mental illness- they are just true to their nature and the kinds of animals they were meant to be, but a narcissist*

is different. They are an extremely disturbed parasite and not the kind of person you'll want any kind of encounter or relationship with.'

Narcissistic abuse is a pervasive pattern of negativity, anger, hate, self-loathing and projection directed at a victim or another person designed to ruin their self-esteem, confuse them, make them doubt their perceptions along with a whole host of other reasons and the consequences are very serious for the victim. Often times, once a narcissist begins devaluing or abusing a victim, the abuse just will not stop, and they will not improve their abuse or go back to being the nicer, doting people they once were.

The abuse will often get worse, and they will continue the pattern further denigrating the victim and then hold them responsible for the narcissist's behavior and leave them feeling dark, depressed, or worthless. Most of the time the narcissist is dealing with their own issues in life, unable to handle them or even if they can, decides to project outward onto this other person and take their anger out on them for other events happening in their own life.

Once the narcissist has chosen to abuse and devalue a target victim, their mind is made up and they rarely are nice to them or treat them with respect, though after periods of extreme lengths of abuse or severe devaluation, or in between episodes of abuse they may throw in love bombing or being doting and nice to the victim in some form and give gifts to them or even just act nice to them in some way putting on a façade of being somewhat of a normal person often fooling the victim.

The victim is often just a mess of internal emotions and trauma bonding to this abuser and has no control over their emotions or feelings and will often just excuse the abuser and continue to maintain somewhat of a cordial relationship with them, though the narcissist may throw in periods of abuse or devaluation while maintaining this relationship in order to strengthen the trauma bond and create more dysfunction.

It's very difficult for a victim to cut off ties with the abuser because this level of abuser has typically traumatized the victim to extreme lengths and in such creative terrifying ways, and even if the victim tries to heal, cope or get away the abuser is there in their life still abusing them, and then being nice to them as well which is the hallmark of the Jekyll Hyde personality of the narcissist.

Initially, the victim was so terrified and shocked by the abuse that was done to them they were unable to get away. The victim may have feared the abuser at some point, initially or still might fear this person. Even after years, it can be very difficult for a victim to get away because this abuser has actually stolen a lot of their power, soul, and energy and they hold this in their energy body and self and has made the victim very weak and unable to be themselves, become strong empowered and get away.

The narcissist's arguments consist only of lies, fabrications, exaggerations, false ideations, projections, minimizing or denying. Nothing they say is the truth and they are remorseless pathological liars of the worst kind.

The narcissists will often employ a large number of tactics in order to destroy their victim's sense of selves and very souls. deny, minimize, blame the victim and gaslight in order to get what they want, win arguments, and shatter and defeat anyone who they may have targeted, victimized, or those who've threatened their false sense of self, questioned or attempted to argue with the narcissist. Destruction is their middle name. Once you are a victim of the narcissist you will have to endure and survive a scenario and situation of major hell and one that just doesn't end.

The narcissist idealizes the victim, then devalues them

The narcissist will often go from valuing the victim to devaluing and abusing them terribly, and the cycle will continue. Once a narcissist begins abusing a victim, there is no mercy involved sadly. The victim will not know what hit them. The narcissist has now devalued that person and victim and they will continue the devaluation cycle, while destroying the victim's self-worth and psyche and every part of the person they can.

The narcissist shows no mercy to the victim and continues this cycle of hatred, negativity, devaluation towards the unsuspecting person who has no clue this person was capable of this kind of evil, hatred and abuse. Once the narcissist disarms the victim with their abuse, they are addicted and refuse to stop. This cycle of abuse, and devaluation will simply continue, and they have now perceived that person to be their personal punching bag, and this cycle of abuse will continue.

Also, a narcissist will not begin abuse on a victim of this nature unless they feel the victim is dependent on them in some form or needs them in some form, and in many cases a dependency is created through all kinds of means, or if the narcissist is a family member or partner, the concept of dependency can be created more easily through all kinds of forms.

Dependency is created by the narcissist through their extreme abuse, destruction of a victim's self-worth and self-esteem and in many more disturbing ways. The narcissist is an adept abuser and does so in various and terrible ways and means. (list the ways a narcissist abuses a victim). Trauma bonding is the means by which and this usually tends to occur, along with Stockholm syndrome of the often perplexed, traumatized and confused victim, who many times will often just side with the abuser, sometimes justify the abuse, or out of sheer horror or fear just be nice to the abuser due to the shock involved with the kind of abuse a narcissist does to their victim.

Common abuse tactics the narcissist uses

The narcissist will implement an array of nasty toxic and abusive tactics towards their victims. This isn't just ordinary abuse being done, it is very extreme and brutal, usually resulting in extreme trauma and shock on the part of the victim:

Gaslighting

Gaslighting is a form of mental abuse in which a perpetrator denies something may have occurred even if there is obvious evidence present, in order to make the victim look or feel crazy, or doubt their own sanity, memory or perception. The narcissist will often use this abuse tactic on a target for a large number of reasons and to also deny the abuse they have done and take no responsibility and attempt to make the victim look and feel crazy

Manipulation

Manipulation is the form of deception that a narcissist uses to commit their evil or atrocious acts. They use many different tactics to employ power and control over their victims, and will often lie and deceive people in many ways to get the desired outcome they want.

Triangulation

The narcissist will often bring a third person in to create chaos and create a dysfunctional scenario in order to make the victim look bad. This is called triangulation where a narcissist uses other people against a victim unfairly

Projection

This is a disordered concept that the narcissist uses to pathologize a victim. They will begin insulting and calling them names or projecting exactly what they are and accusing the victim of this very thing. It's something that seems to be done through the very lens of their disorder and they seem to have no concept that they are projecting their own flaws and characteristics onto someone else.

Projective identification

This is a common abuse tactic used by a narcissist to project their own internal feelings onto a victim through different means, which in turn causes the victim to project or act out that feeling or concept back onto the abuser or just in general, or to feel this way themselves.

If a narcissist is feeling dark depressed and down internally or if they feel a particular way about something, they will often end up attacking the target and in turn will ensure that the target feels this same way now about the particular event or thing.

Narcissistic rage

This is the hate-filled rage that a narcissist subjects to a victim usually full of extreme anger, insults, hatred and huge attacks. It is very hostile and toxic in nature and is of a specific kind. Many narcissists will rage at victims in extreme ways subjecting them to unnecessary abuse and pain.

Usually, the narcissist is just taking their anger out on a victim unnecessarily and in order to purge any inner feelings they have since they lack the ability to internalize feelings in a healthy way. They also rage out at victims because of life events or things that happen in their life that they can't handle, are stressed out about or might be negative to them.

Narcissistic injury

This is a specific type of injury done to a narcissist by a victim- usually when a victim somehow is able to speak the truth about this abuser, or insult them in some form. The narcissist will get injured by this, and it may be a huge blow to their life, or their reality in some form.

Narcissistic injury usually results in more hostile abuse being done to the victim by the abuser, who cannot handle what was said to them or can't handle their own psyche. They may resort to even more extreme abuse as their disordered way of counteracting the injury that was done to their ego or self.

Narcissistic reactions

The narcissist often abuses the victim in order to get reactions out of them. This is called narcissistic supply and they use this supply as some kind of mechanism they feed off of, or a supposed need they have due to their disorder. Many narcissists will resort to extreme amounts of abuse or different tactics in order to get the most creative, negative or emotion filled reactions from the victim.

Crazy-making

The narcissist will often gaslight their victim, or make them appear to themselves or to others to be crazy in some form, irrational or unstable. They will resort to abrasive tactics to destabilize a victim's internal sense of self and their own belief system and perceptions in order to do this

Devaluation

This is a phase, or time of abuse when a narcissist looks down upon the victim and attacks them with many various hazardous forms of painful and traumatic narcissistic abuse tactics. The narcissist will often idealize a victim, and then devalue them and continue with this cycle confusing and causing them a great amount of angst and trauma internally.

Smear campaigns and slander

The narcissist will often employ horrible smear campaigns against their victim usually when a victim is not suspecting this kind of behavior or to discredit or destroy their reputation. The narcissist will go around to friends, family members or whoever they can and spread malicious lies and rumors about the narcissist in a disturbing way.

The victim is often left shattered, broken, confused and doesn't have many people to turn to for support as a result of this kind of abuse. The narcissist or victim's friends or family will often side with the narcissist, rather than helping out the distraught victim.

Minimizing

This is an abusive tactic by which a narcissist or abuser minimizes the horrific abuse they have done to a victim, and makes it seem as if it's really not that significant, the victim is overreacting or overthinking things. Statements such as "you're just too emotional" is a form of minimizing of abuse or "nothing wrong was done, that wasn't a big deal, you're blowing it out of proportion" are ways a narcissist not only deflects the blame off them, but in their sick delusional mind just pretends the abuse didn't exist, or blames it on the victim being irrational, overemotional, stupid etc.

Denying

This is a tactic a narcissist uses against the victim by flat out denying the abuse ever occurred, changing the story, pathologically lying about what happened, and even blaming the victim for making up lies by claiming none of what the victim is stating ever happened.

Victim blaming

This is a very sad tactic a narcissist uses to constantly pathologize the victim and rather than to admit their own actions, they will blame the victim for their own abuse towards the victim, and for many other things as well. The narcissist will often pathologize a victim in a secretive or even open way when others are around in order to make the victim look like the perpetrator, and to take any blame off of them.

Love-bombing

This is an abuse tactic a narcissist uses when a victim is possibly threatening to leave them or get away, or when a narcissist decides they want to value the victim and treat them with kindness. They will often love bomb them with nice things, gifts and other things showing great adulation and love towards them. They do this with the attempts to amend the situation between and to fool the victim into thinking they have feelings for them or want everything to be ok, or a way to apologize for the devaluation phase that just happened. This continues in a cycle of abuse with the narcissist.

Narcissists want it all

Narcissists want it all. A narcissist could have everything- a relationship, children, money, lots of friends- they could have a dream life that anyone might want yet they still will steal take from and destroy those who do not have this life or the things they have. They only want to make sure of one thing- that their victim who they stole everything from in some way never has the life they have- it's one of the few ways they are there to make sure their victim is never above them or has more than them.

The victim or target of a narcissist has become nothing more than a punching bag of a narcissist, there solely as the scapegoat- to be used to pin the narcissist's anger, hate and sins on in the most hostile way possible, and as an object for the narcissist to lash out at when the disordered narcissist needs this.

A narcissist will destroy you and steal your energy and they will continue doing this even if they possess an abundance of your energy. They will always want more- especially if it's something they once started, it's now something they just will not stop. Narcissists want to take everything from their victim, crush and destroy them beyond belief, leave them with anger, angst, agony, pain, trauma, torment, loneliness and no hope and continue this cycle as long as they are in any form of contact with the victim or until the end of time.

As long as the victim has positivity, a great spirit or some hope and something to destroy or steal, the narcissist will make sure to take it and more and more and they just will not stop. The narcissistic cycle of abuse really doesn't end. The narcissist might have periods of valuation, love bombing and forms of positive reinforcement in between all the harrowing negativity and abuse they torment their victims with, but that's just to ensure that the twisted trauma bond they have developed, and unhealthy bonding gets stronger and more dysfunctionally developed by the confused narcissist who is such a disordered creature.

Narcissists are extremely devious, cunning and calculating in their actions and abuse towards others. They embark on the most heinous smear campaigns against their targets, they destroy lives without a single thought, they press charges on a victim just for sport, they ruin lives just because they're bored and have a need to destroy and take their anger out on someone or something. They plan and calculate their behaviors in the most outrageous ways to effectively steal your energy, time, and life in any possible way they can, or destroy you internally so that you are unable to function or cope.

Narcissists want their targets to be depleted financially, emotionally, socially and in any way they're able to do so. They will resort to extremes such as committing crimes covertly to get the desired result they want- the victim ruined completely, and dependent on the narcissist in some form. They want the victim to be weak, unable to cope so they can further denigrate and destroy them and continue this vicious destructive cycle.

The Narcissist steals and destroys lives

You will often sadly find the narcissist surrounded by a network of very positive, normal, kind people helping and supporting them in every aspect of their lives in a deep and shallow way, while the victims of the narcissist generally are surrounded only by the narcissist and a small or non-existent support group, and other abusers or narcissists or lower vibration people.

This is because the narcissist has stolen the victim's power, destroyed them completely and made sure they are completely isolated from others for many reasons (fear, guilt, intimidation (feeling as if they aren't worthy or good enough of others or as if others haven't been through what they have and have normal good lives), stolen power and energy, depression, sadness and just total isolation. The narcissist has almost created a hierarchy chart now which is the sadly the victim's life, with the narcissist being on top and the victim being on the very bottom with nothing underneath.

The narcissist is also in desperate need of narcissistic supply- which is adulation, adoration, affection and is usually surrounded by a plethora and network of admirers or people who feed the narcissist in some form. They will have an abundance of friends, admirers, or many people who they have groomed in some form, in order to feel superior or liked, and have even used these people in many ways against the victim.

They will often become more and more empowered from destroying the victim, and mostly steal the victim's energy or power and use it to elevate themselves and their own happiness and gain a larger support system, all while creating extreme dysfunction in the victim, so that they are abused, shamed, ridiculed, chastised, and become terrified of living in the normal world, or too afraid to make friendships or bonds or are just unable to due to all the abuse being done to them. You will often find the narcissist having many friends, while the victim becomes isolated and has no one any longer.

The victim's life is very similar to a hierarchy chart, where the narcissist has repressed and suppressed and destroyed the victim's very life experiences, soul, and even spiritual life or journey, and spiritually is holding the victim hostage in some way in life and others are energetically unable to enter the victim's life, unless they are unhealthy or toxic to them in some way.

The narcissist is at the top of the chart, with numerous friends, family and lovers, above the victim, while they have stolen everything from them and are above them just crushing them. I often say that a narcissist has stolen family, friends and usually their life from their victim, while the narcissist many times has it all- family, friends, and often will have more than the victim does socially and in other forms. Many times, the narcissist will purposely steal friends or new potential friends from their victim, by jumping in and isolating them, being friends with the person first, or finding ways of sabotaging potential friends right away.

The victim may not be stuck in a home, or a room kidnapped, but the sad truth is the narcissist has hijacked their life and has taken over, and there is a lot of trauma energy present from all the abnormal abuse a victim has been through, and others don't resonate with the darkness and trauma energy present within the abuse victim and it becomes difficult to find or meet people because of this.

The victim's energy is stolen from them, their soul and self-esteem has become repressed and destroyed and disordered, and they will tend to unconsciously or energetically project a whole range of emotions or feelings to others, which others may be unable to handle or fully understand.

Narcissists often have a strong support system and have been glorified or supported by many others

Most of the time, narcissists have been glorified and adored by others, especially their golden children and those who are in their lives and give them a constant supply of narcissistic supply. They have been enabled by the other narcissistic parent or their spouse or partner, friends' family and others. No one has really stopped the narcissism and they have ensured this.

They create and develop these very sources of supply and make sure they will only be beneficial for the narcissist- to ease their pain or sorrows, be of comfort to them if they need it, or are there for them only and to use against the victim any way they can. As they age, they only get worse because these abusive patterns have become deeply ingrained in them, and they refuse to accept or believe they are doing anything wrong or just don't care. They were never told to stop this behavior or chastised for it in any way by others friends or family and it is a repeat cycle of disturbed behavior will continue.

If they are married and have this negative family dynamic, their spouse is often abusive in nature too and will join or support their behavior or turn into an enabler- enable their actions and just not stop them from harming the victims.

Narcissists may have friends but most of the time, they don't care for their friends. Some genuinely have normal bonds with them or friendships and others are used as narcissistic supply or objects to the narcissist- it simply depends upon their personal disorder because every situation and disorder has varying complexities.

The narcissist isolates a victim and destroys relationships

Often times, the narcissist will isolate the victim through their extreme negative patterns of abuse and abuse or trauma victims often feel helpless, alone, powerless, shattered, unable to deal with their situation, extreme guilt, and unable to tell anyone about what is happening to them due to fear, guilt, or judgment. The kind of abuse done by the narcissist is meant to destroy a victim in the most harrowing of ways and many end up being silent victims so distraught by their own situation, gasping for air almost, and trying desperately to get away from the abuse being done to them or heal from it in some way. It's usually not something you can describe to others and most of the time others seem to be indifferent or be unable to react to the situation or be of any help.

The narcissist will also destroy relationships, family relationships and any relationship they're able to of the victim if it's in their power. The narcissist might pick a fight with the victim, before a family member or friend is going to visit, and anger them in some form making them look bad, or may even continue with the fight while the family member is there and insult the victim, in order to make 'them' look bad, aggressive in some form, to other family members or friends rather than allowing them to have peace or a good time. The narcissist will often slander a person to family, friends or others making up all kinds of crazy stories in order to further isolate them from close family or friends.

The narcissist wants to destroy a victim's life and then ensure they are unable to get help from others and will continue what is known as a smear campaign or slander against a victim.

Often, a victim is shocked because the narcissist was somewhat of a close trusted friend, partner, family member, co-worker, or someone the narcissist trusted in some sense, even if they did some kind of evil or heinous act towards that person. That person definitely wasn't expecting a deep-rooted smear campaign against the target victim on top of all of the abuse that was already done.

No one will ever stop the narcissist from their abuse or actions, it's quite shocking.

The narcissist doesn't want the victim to heal or progress

The narcissist wants everyone to destroy the victim. The narcissist employs such abusive tactics that a victim is destroyed within, and their self-esteem ruined, and others or other abusers often take advantage of them or abuse them too. This further erodes a victim's self-esteem and makes it very difficult to heal and forces the abuser to be surrounded with toxic people in their life, rather than healthy positive or beneficial people.

The narcissist doesn't want the victim to heal or get help, their rigorous dangerous abuse is done so in a matter in which abuse victims will often end up victims of many others and it becomes a repeat cycle or pattern. The narcissist wants to make sure that their abuse causes extreme amounts of damage to a person, and so that person just isn't able to cope or heal and becomes other people's target as well.

The narcissist also employs varieties of smear campaigns against a victim, and maligns and slanders them to others, ensuring they're unable to get help from others, further devaluing and ruining their life and reputation and usually shocking the victim with this behavior.

The narcissist does this for a number of reasons along with part of their disorder of projection- rather than take responsibility for their evil acts, they pin it all on the victim making them seem crazy, unstable, or as if something is wrong with them. They also want to further discredit the victim to others or their sanity, and make it seem as if they are full of issues amongst other things. The victim is then usually alone with no one to turn to as friends and family have been fed mistruths and fabrications about them.

Chapter 4

Trauma bonding and co-dependency

Trauma-bonding with a narcissist

Trauma bonding is when an individual becomes emotionally attached to someone who has caused them pain.

It can happen in any type of relationship, but is often seen in relationships with narcissists.

Trauma bonds are characterized by intermittent reinforcement, where the narcissist will give just enough positive attention to make sure their partner doesn't leave.

They occur gradually over the course of seven stages that keep the victim in an endless cycle of manipulation and abuse. Trauma-bonding is also an energetic attachment created by repeated abuse, along with being saved every now and then, or showered with a little bit of positive reinforcement to further destroy and confuse the victim, and make the bond become stronger and deeper.

This type of conditioning is intuitively exploited by narcissists. They are masters at giving us just enough and then ripping it all away. In conjunction with gaslighting, emotional abuse and manipulation designed to make us question our reality, the major building blocks for trauma-bonding are formed.

Trauma bonds are extremely unhealthy, strange and destructive ties that are created by an abuser or narcissist with a victim and done so in a very carefully crafted, hostile way in order to leave the victim disarmed, disabled, and unable to cope with the scenario and in a state of mind of not feeling or being themselves, and being confused victims who are now prone to this kind of unhealthy tie or bonding mechanism.

Trauma bonds are one very manipulative, evil and sick way for a narcissistic abuser to destroy their targets or those who they have chosen as victims. The narcissist's abuse isn't well thought out, secretive covert abuse. It is extremely hostile, soul shattering and character maligning, out in the open abuse that will generally ruin and destroy a person's self-esteem and very core.

The narcissist's abuse is typically very malignant, dangerous, angry, full of hostility and rage and will create not just one or a few aspects of trauma bonding, but will usually create hundreds of sad and disturbing trauma bonds within the confused, traumatized victim who is incapable of even handling a single aspect of the nature of their abuse much less many varying kinds. The narcissist will not just create a few destructive trauma bonds between themselves and the victim, they will make sure to create numerous damaging trauma bonds in order to make sure that the victim will never be able to recover, cope with or heal or do away with this unnatural, unhealthy type of bonding.

The trauma bond is usually created when the narcissist does extreme abuse to a victim and begins to ruin them internally. It's an energetic dysfunctional bond created from extreme trauma and abuse and holds the experiences the victim had to go through and the trauma energy present there but worse, the narcissist will carry the energy of the victim and the victim will often feel empty, lifeless and drained lacking in energy and worse just a mess of disordered feelings and emotions due to the abuse of the narcissist being subjected upon them.

The narcissist will often turn the victim into a mess of disorder and trauma energy and will usually very adeptly do so using their strange disorder, and in turn will transform or attempt to transform you into what they are deep inside- a monster lurking within an angry, grotesque, diseased, dark, morbid creature with a frail angry confused childlike ego yearning to lash out at the world for their life not being the way they expected it to be. But they will be unable to do so because you have a spirit and soul that shines bright through. They will try their hardest to destroy you and they might, but because you are a normal person unlike them, you might be able to bounce back from the madness they engulf you with.

Their mid-life crisis will become your worst nightmare, their stress over any little thing will become a bad day for you, and they refuse to stop the darkness they project onto others especially their victims the ones who've been scapegoated by these monsters who bear the burdens of the very evils they commit against them.

Trauma bonds are made up of emotional mental psychological and energetic ideations based on the abuse that was done to a victim. Psychologically a victim has become damaged from the type of abuse the narcissist is doing to them as well as the narcisssist projecting their own feelings and emotions and energies onto them. There is a spiritual component involved as well usually and a lot of negative energy involved.

The narcissist will use all types of abuse tactics in order to effectively trauma bond with their victim. There are seven known common stages of trauma bonding which include:

- Idealization- During the idealization phase, the abuser portrays themselves as the perfect partner. They shower the victim with love, affection, and attention, making them feel special and cherished. This stage creates a sense of euphoria and establishes a strong emotional connection between the victim and the abuser.

- Devaluation- In the devaluation phase, the abuser begins to exhibit controlling and manipulative behaviors. They may criticize, belittle, or demean the victim, causing them to question their self-worth. The abuser alternates between moments of affection and cruelty, leaving the victim confused and emotionally vulnerable.

- Cognitive Dissonance: Cognitive dissonance is a psychological term that describes the mental conflict experienced by the victim during the trauma bonding process. They may have conflicting thoughts and emotions about the abuser, simultaneously recognizing the abuse while still holding onto positive memories and feelings.

- Traumatic events: The traumatic events that occurred within the relationship play a role in trauma bonding. They can be physical, emotional, or psychological in nature and strengthen the bond between victim and the abuser.

- The Deterioration of the inner self: The victim's sense of self gradually deteriorates. They may lose confidence, feel helpless and question their own judgment. The abuser's manipulation tactics and constant criticism erode the victim's self-esteem making them more dependent on the abuser for validation.

- Dependence and Isolation: The victim becomes increasingly dependent on the abuser for emotional or even physical survival. The abuser isolates the victim from friends, family and other sources of support creating a sense of powerlessness and reinforcing the trauma bond.

- Breaking Free: Breaking free from trauma bonding is essential towards a person's self-healing and growth. It requires recognizing the abusive nature of the relationship, seeking professional help and establishing a support system. With time and support, victims can regain their autonomy and rebuild their lives.

How the narcissist creates a co-dependency with the victim:

The narcissist generally creates a co-dependency with the victim and forces the victim to feel as if they need this person. The truth is, the narcissist is the one who needs the person, but more so in a sense that they need someone to unleash their rage out on and a permanent punching bag. They want to project every feeling they have internally onto their victim and turn the victim into what they are, when the victim was happy, healthy, and normal beforehand.

If the narcissist felt miserable, empty, and lonely, they will implement abuse tactics so that the victim now feels this way. The narcissist never admits to themselves, or to the person they need them for any reason, and it's usually because the narcissist doesn't want to be alone in many cases, or is alone and that person is someone who might be considered to be close to them- a friend or family member.

The narcissist will further punish the victim for them needing them in any way, and continue with the cycle of abuse. They will continue devaluing the victim, something they will do for a long time to come. Co-dependency can be emotional, familial, or financial in nature along with many other factors, however one of the main factors besides material ones is the fact that the narcissist has stolen a significant portion of the victim's energy and power and holds that within themselves, and continues stealing this power from them and makes sure to keep projecting negative emotions and energies onto them, so that the victim loses their inner self and soul in huge ways.

The narcissist creates this co-dependency and neediness on the abuser by resorting to extreme forms of abuse toward the victim, and the victim is unable to cope with it. The narcissist who was once a supportive, kind person to the victim might be someone who the victim already may need in their life in a minor way, and will pick fights with them, abuse them, gaslight, give the silent treatment and destabilize the relationship creating a hostile manic unstable frightening environment where there are fights and anger and where there is uncertainty.

The victim is often frightened that the narcissist will not be in their life again or speak to them again, and they will resort to an internal neediness that is generally automatically created, and in many ways is also of an energetic nature. Often times, the victim is feeling the narcissist's own energy and feelings, and it's the narcissist who is generally in fear of losing control over this person or even losing this person.

Many times, the narcissist resorts to extreme abuse tactics in order to destroy a victim's life or take the abuse further suddenly, because they have ulterior motives- they may be secretly wanting to cause more harm to the victim and have a plan at hand. The victim often knows this and may even be in fear of their life for what the narcissist might desire to do to them. Many times, the narcissist is losing control of their own mind and life, and then will attempt to gain control by traumatizing and ruining the victim's life.

The narcissist tortures, destroys and traumatizes the victim using hostile erratic methods, so that the victim can trauma bond and in turn, go through extreme emotional and energetic interactions within themselves or around them and end up feeling as if they need the narcissist. they feel this way for a variety of reasons and also because they feel very weak since they have been destroyed and have had their energy and life force stolen from them in the most vindictive cruelest ways possible.

The victim feels they are dependent on the narcissist

The narcissist wants the victim to feel a dependence or need for them, and then they further punish the victim for feeling this way even fi they don't fully, and if the victim doesn't feel this way anymore or are gaining some kind of confidence or strength, the narcissist will make sure to continue abusing them terribly in order to make sure they are still broken and in need of the narcissist mentally, emotionally, or energetically.

You are not really dependent on the narcissist- you only believe you are. That is because, the concept of co-dependency is a lie. You might be financially dependent on the narcissist in some form, or dependent on them for other physical or worldly means, but mentally and psychologically and in other ways, you do not hold any form of dependence upon this person. The narcissist has created a false belief and feeling within a victim through extreme emotional and energetic trauma.

The narcissist will break the victim down so the victim is weak destroyed traumatized and feels as if they need the narcissist. The narcissist will create a false and real sense of dependency. The victim is usually so destroyed they experience extreme amounts of trauma and may be unable to cope or even function and will hold extreme amounts of trauma energy.

The narcissist wants a victim to be weak and mentally emotionally and energetically dependent on them. They never want the person to heal, only to suffer and be in mental, emotional and physical pain.

Most victims of narcissists become broken, weak people in need of support and healing

Many victims of narcissistic abuse might seem like codependents, but the real truth is they have often just been broken down in such extreme ways, it is difficult for them to cope or even function most of the time. The narcissist might be a caretaker, a family member, a partner, or anyone in their life who is primary to them or even often exclusive, so the victim believes they feel a dependency on this person for a variety of reasons, none of which are usually very valid except for potential financial dependency.

The narcissist creates an illusion of dependency

They aren't necessarily dependent on the narcissist- that is a disturbing illusion usually created due to the abuse of the narcissist being so harsh and severe and the internal and mental damage that they have undergone.

The narcissist was a figure in their lives most of the time, who seemed as if they played a necessary role in the victims life and they ingrained a false concept that the victim has some need for this person.

The concept of needing the abuser comes from the long drawn out nature of severe toxic abuse, all the various emotions and dysfunctional energies involved, and the breaking down of the victims internal self and stealing their power and energy and filling it with such dysfunction. The abuser usually holds the energy or power of the victim, and this is why the victim feels a sense of this false need for the abuser.

Most victims of narcissistic abuse aren't codependents or of that nature. They often have encountered many different kinds of narcissists and the patterns of abuse seem to constantly manifest in their lives. They have been in numerous abusive relationships or situations, and the pattern seems to continually occur. They are often overwhelmed by the sheer amount of abuse they have had to endure, and most people do not possess the faculties to handle this amount or level of anything like this.

Some are of a positive high energy and negative broken people will gravitate towards them to take their energy, or try to heal from them but in a negative and toxic way. Many disordered and unhealthy people will drawn to them and other negative abusive people will attempt to take advantage of them.

Part of the reason a person feels a codependent is energetic in nature is because of energy. They hold your energy and power within themselves and in many other forms. They will even steal a victim's life force and purposely or unintentionally use it to strengthen their friends family or others, so their lives are benefited while the victims life is destroyed.

Most victims of Narcissistic abuse are just broken, weak people in need of severe healing and help because often, especially in the beginning stages of narcissistic abuse, they will be unable to get away from the abuser. They may want to or try but the abuser will usually employ tactics to keep them around or under their thumb. This is how most narcissists tend to function in their frightening toxic relationships. They usually will not let the person get away at first, and will continue to destroy them as much as they can.

Chapter 5

The Victims of the Narcissist

Characteristics of a Narcissist's victims

Abuse victims learn to cultivate unhealthy dysfunctional relationships and will often have a poor sense of confidence, self-esteem, and broken and damaged boundaries. Even if they are confident, radiating charismatic individuals, they will lack proper and healthy boundaries and accept in some way those who may not be right for them or those who may be abusive towards them in any form.

Some abuse victims are so confused they will compare, and contrast abuse types based on what was done to them in the past, and even accept or put up with other forms of abuse simply because they are already dealing with abuse that may seem worse, or they may not want to be stuck with their abusers only, so they'll take some other person who isn't the narcissist or abuser.

The narcissist's victims will generally end up being a vast plethora of varying types of people, however they will often choose people who present the traits of kindness, goodness, sensitivity, empathy, intelligence, and people who may even be high energy or possess traits that are empowering, great, superior or even those of weakness (such as people with mental illnesses, the weak, old, formerly abused).

The narcissist might choose a person with the best and brightest personality, those with the best qualities or the most potential as their victims, in order to do the most damage to these people, destroying their current and future lives and making sure the victim is destroyed for years or decades to come. The narcissists's abuse is extreme and does not end. The narcissist is a master at destroying a person's psyche, sense of self and self-worth, self-esteem.

Once the victim is destroyed, they will be full of weakness, trauma energy, and will often have fresh emotional and psychological wounds present, which will make them very easy prey for any other abusers, narcissists and others. Often, the narcissist will shatter a person's very boundaries, and after shattering those boundaries, will continue on with this cycle, until there is really nothing left of a victim.

The narcissist will in every way possible destroy every relationship a victim has with every healthy person, in very overt and covert ways, until there is no one left except the narcissist for help, to rely on and so the narcissist can continue to objectify and destroy the victim. The narcissist purposely destroys the victims, shatters their very core, sense of self and boundaries so that they lose their self-esteem completely and become the most easy targeted prey for other abusers, narcissists and for everyone.

Victims are often surrounded by other abusers or narcissists

The narcissists victims will often be surrounded by a number of abusers, toxic people, weak people looking to feed off the victim as well who may possess traits of narcissism within them, and all kinds of people wanting to take advantage of this person. The narcissists victim will often be surrounded by toxic people, and they will continue to be the victim after a very long time- that is because the narcissist designed their abuse to occur for this very reason and for this to happen to the unsuspecting confused victim.

The abuse they did to this victim wasn't just done once or twice, or even ten times- it has become a pattern done hundreds or thousands of time, that the narcissist does to this person in order to disarm their boundaries and sense of self-worth, shatter their very soul, and destroy their self-esteem for good. The narcissist's abuse simply never ends.

If the narcissist senses that their carefully controlled abused and used victim is gaining any form of power or control, sense of self-worth of their own or crawling out of the hole they dumped this person is, the narcissist will very forcefully make sure to continue the abuse and cycle and even make it worse and make sure the victim is back down in the hole of abuse and terror this terrorist narcissist wants them to be in and has carefully controlled and made sure of.

The narcissists victims may be some of the strongest and most intelligent, resilient people out there; however, they are simply unable to handle the abuse, manipulation, gaslighting, smear campaigns, overt and covert madness and torment and even torture the narcissist will do to these innocent victims who are disarmed and thrown off and then ultimately destroyed by. The narcissists' victim isn't just an ordinary abuse victim being brought down, abused, gaslighted, or destroyed, they are being destroyed by the most destructive creation, the narcissist himself, the most disordered creation of a personality disorder and disorder itself.

Narcissists turn their victims into punching bags

The narcissist has turned this healthy, loving, kind, caring, giving, once confident individual, into a mess of confusion, hatred, revenge-seeking person who has nowhere to turn to, and has no clue how to help themselves or deal with the trauma this monster is causing them to deal with. The narcissist has chosen its victim unwisely, and generally will choose the most loving, caring individual for this is whom the narcissist can gain the most from, prey upon easily, who is most vulnerable to the narcissists extreme abuse.

They will tend to choose the most sensitive prey, those with extreme ration, intellect, who will be the most damaged out of anyone, and even the person who cares for the narcissist the most. They do this to steal the most from their victims- all the qualities and traits the narcissist does not possess, or traits they may have once possessed in their life at a younger, and traits they wish to possess.

The narcissist wishes they were like their victims or were their victims, but simply can't be them. Often times, the victims will possess the good and great qualities the narcissist wishes they truly had or that they once possessed but that cease to exist now due to their very disorder, or other external factors, even other abusers or narcissists that may have stolen these traits from them through their own abuse.

They want the harm and damage done to be the greatest and have the most impact from which they can gain the most results and reactions from, and they want to mold and shape the victim into a punching bag for the narcissist, devoid of their own feelings and beliefs and sense of self-worth and want them to turn into an object solely for the narcissist to abuse, demean, destroy and objectify- the narcissist's personal punching bag, which is what the narcissistic abuse victim becomes, rather than being their normal, healthy, happy self.

The victim will simply go from being a happy, healthy, confident, or normal enough person to a projection bag for the narcissist. The narcissist will use the victim to project all of their inner hatred, self-loathing, rage and disdain for others onto the victim or victims. The narcissist is generally an extremely unhappy person who is not happy with their current situation in life. They have carefully and even with extreme disorder, chaos, and anger crafted the victim or victims into being pillars of abuse for this creature and not much else. This cycle will continue until the victim gets away from the narcissist, minimizes or avoids contact, or until the narcissist agrees to get therapy for the situation, which rarely ever happens.

The narcissist usually needs the victim in some form

Often times, the narcissist holds a false belief that the victim needs the narcissist, which truly isn't really the case. The narcissist has denigrated, abused and devalued this person treating them like nothing more than a punching bag for the narcissists's woes, problems, internal issues, anger, hate for others, disagreements with others, arguments, humiliations, evil actions etc, and in turn will either or not create a dependency or believe there is a co-dependency going on with the victim, however this isn't always the case. The victim usually doesn't need the narcissist, it's usually the other way around.

The narcissist generally needs the victim in some form and decides as usual to distort it and twist it all around using their sick techniques of projection and projective identification, and will create a false sense of co-dependency between they and the victim, and forces the victim to suffer greatly, and then in turn falsely feel they need the narcissist in some form, or that they can't exist or live without the narcissist. The reality is, it's the narcissist that felt that way about the victim initially and still does- until they have devaluded and discarded the narcissist, something they do very often.

They will usually punish the victim for being in a co-dependent situation with the narcissist, being underneath the narcissist as they believe somewhere inside themselves the person is, and will further abuse the target. Needing a person isn't a normal healthy habit or trait one has in a relationship.

People may feel they need each other a healthy loving way, that involves love and positive interactions, but narcissists create this unhealthy concept of needing someone, using their disordered abilities and their disturbing abuse such as projection, which they use to throw their own feelings onto the victim, and projective identification and they in turn force the victim to turn into what the narcissist is- someone who has that unhealthy abnormal feeling of needing someone in an unhealthy toxic way.

The struggles victims must endure

It's difficult for a victim to witness some person who destroyed their life and did heinous unforgivable things to them being so nice to others or giving them gifts and never abusing them. They often help others out and lift them up. It adds to the anger and inner turmoil present in an abuse victim. I often say my family members friends are all successful because the family member never destroyed their life, however they did mine. It's a difficult concept for an abuse victim to grasp though of course those people may have had their own struggles but most didn't.

They just weren't destroyed by the monster that did so much confusing abuse to the victim, that the victim was unable to succeed or cope with the abuse or move on and heal and form healthy relationships. The family members that hurt my life were there to support and bring up their friends and family and others and never hurt or interfered in their life in a negative way, only mine. And yet, they seem to be the only people present in my life, which is often the case with victims of abuse. Their abusers are the only ones present just to continue the mistreatment andwill make sure the victim just doesn't progress.

Those who destroy lives should be held accountable in some form, especially narcissists. There should be a way there has to be, but there isn't so as a result, the victim has to resort to being mistreated terrorized by this creature permanently if they can't get away, and their life ruined in many forms.

The victim is often alone with mental health professionals usually misunderstanding narcissism or their difficult situations and even gaslighting, confusing, or blaming them for the abuse further destroying them internally damaging them, and not allowing them to gain the support they so desperately need or the healing that is necessary in order for them to gain even some strength within themselves.

This causes the healing process to go backwards, further ruining a victim's psyche, soul, and world. Many others like the narcissist will further pathologize the victim, destroying their self-esteem even more and they will barely or never be able to heal at all.

Victims often feel shame deep seated guilt for the abuse, fear of judgments, fear something is wrong with them, fear social interactions, their life is generally destroyed and their perception of life and people changes.

They carry with them various negative energies that might draw in other negative or unhealthy people and relationships especially predators because they can sense how wounded these victims are.

Victims often experience health issues, extreme anxiety, social anxiety, feel their world or life is crumbling, destabilization, internalization of their feelings, unresolved trauma, internal pain, extreme confusion, inability to think straight, dizziness, exhaustion, fatigue, anger, revenge, or resentment.

Victims of abuse are full of chaotic energies and trauma energy

Victims of abuse have very frightening, toxic trauma energy that is filled with the narcissist's negativity and when boundaries have been shattered and trauma bonds have been created, others can sense this dysfunction in some form, and this strange weakness that seems to be present, and will often use it to target a victim, or further abuse them as well.

They may be unable to be around the victim due to all the chaotic energy present, and may be unable to understand or resonate with what they have no clue is happening. Narcissists and abusers seek to do this very thing to a victim, so that they are unable to gain strength, get help and become isolated from others, and so others too will resort to treating them differently or in a negative way as well. Narcissists expect others to do the abuse to the victim, and for the abuse to last for a long time, and this is the disturbing tactic they employ towards victims, in order to produce these results.

The victim is usually very weak, has lost a sense of control in their life, has dysfunctional energy and emotions within them, is full of chaotic trauma energy, is unable to regain any form of their power or strength, and may even develop forms of chronic fatigue due to physical issues residing within them because of the abuse they are enduring.

Abusers often silence their victims and then leave them to be silenced or mistreated by others. Victims often withdraw, may turn into introverts, become quiet, scared, passive, are unable to handle or cope with the trauma, and aren't sure who or where to turn to.

Many times they have turned to family or friends, who don't reciprocate any form or care or love towards them or act indifferent or aren't sure how to react to their situation. Victims may appear shy or weak to others, when they are really very traumatized people who need healing from the situation or experiences they have had to endure.

Many victims become overly kind, nice, turn into people pleasers, fear other people's abuse or repercussions, and often feel others have an upper hand over them or are above them in some or many ways. They feel others are strong, healthy and happy while they are abused and weak compared to them. Many are also overly apologetic or are constantly apologizing in their interactions because the abuser has eroded their sense of self-worth.

Many victims of abuse will suffer from physical conditions such as chronic fatigue, anxiety, mental disorders, confusion, lack of confidence, lack of strength, physical ailments, and other problems which arise as a result of the negative emotional and physical terror that has been done to them by the pathological narcissist.

Victims of abuse feel powerless

Abuse victims generally have repressed and unresolved trauma, have been through so much trauma, and negativity, they may doubt their own selves, decisions, their self-worth and even develop social anxieties and may find it difficult to be around with, or interact with others. They may feel shock, guilt, grief, anger, depression, confusion, sadness, and may not resonate with most people and are unable to form healthy bonds or relationships with others.

They will often feel like others, or no one is going through or has been through what they have, and others seem so happy and healthy and normal, and they haven't heard stories of this level or nature of abuse from anyone they know, so they will resort to isolating themselves from others and feeling different and out of place.

The friends of the narcissist aren't going through anything like this, neither are their own friends, or anyone they have ever known usually. The truth is, there are hundreds of and thousands of victims of narcissists out there and if you end up on the internet and forums you will read very similar stories of others who have been through this nature of abuse by a narcissist, and stories that will be far worse than your own.

Even if they don't feel this way or have recovered from the abuse in some form, they may still need to fully heal somewhere deep within, in order to be able to meet healthy people and form good relationships with others, or to develop a normal social life. The constant depletion of their energy, taking of their power, and dysfunction being lashed out onto them by the abuser ensures they will doubt their own selves, have self-esteem issues, and develop many negative feelings towards what is occurring and have a dismal outlook on life. Many are depressed, feeling hopeless, confused, unsure of how to handle the situation.

A victim of a narcissist really is that- a powerless victim who is desperately trying to survive the trauma and abuse being done to them and hoping to escape it or hoping it ends. I wish a victim was an empowered individual and they are as a living being, and human but upon encountering the disordered narcissist they become prey for this predator and disordered dangerous creature which can be compared to a sociopath psychopath or any other vicious predator out there in society. Victims often become broken, disordered, weak people in need of serious healing and trauma therapy.

Narcissists seek permanent victims

Narcissists attack and destroy their victims not only so the victims can become current and future permanent targets of the narcissist, but so that the victim can become everybody's target as well. The victim will end up losing their confidence, sense of self, be so destroyed and shattered that they won't be able to function or cope in everyday life and interactions between others in the victim's life will be ruined too. The narcissist seeks to destroy every relationship the target has in the most disarraying way possible. This is the ultimate goal of the narcissist- to turn their targets into permanent victims for anyone, make them more vulnerable and prone to abuse.

Narcissists exploit their victims very self and soul making them lifelong targets of any person out there, and this is how they do the most damaging and dangerous ultimate exploitation of their targets. Their targets are now just walking fresh wounds for not only predators to attack and take advantage of but for everyone to do the same.

The narcissist caused this to happen to the target intentionally and was the very reason they did the kind of abuse they did to this particular victim. The narcissist wants to make sure you never succeed and become everyone's punching bag, not just theirs and hold the identity of punching bag in your fragile, weak confused, now distraught mind and feel this way forever.

However, even this outcome for the target of the narcissist isn't enough for this confused damaged and disordered individual to want to stop- they will continue their abuse and the cycle of narcissistic abuse towards their victims for as long as they can and so long as the victim is down and weak now and as long as they are now an easy target for the narcissistic after being destroyed in thousands of ways.

The narcissist gets more evil and mentally ill with age. The elderly don't become old nice people and grow out of their old age- they turn into more dysfunctional monsters and will go through phases where their abuse gets worse and worse.

Who do Narcissists Target?

The narcissist often might be someone who is your best friend or who has done many nice things for you. They may be helping you out financially and may have created an abnormal dependence on them or some form of dependence.

You might wonder- why did the narcissist choose you, and not the neighbor, the stranger, the distant relative or even their close relative to be evil or abusive towards and to unleash their wrath upon? Well, the reason the narcissist chose you is because an abuser can't choose someone who isn't very close to them or someone distant in any form- that person won't be affected by their abuse and will be able to get away fast. They also are generally cowards and fake people and can't abuse anyone or display any form of anything that is negative or harsh towards others, only their victims.

They will expose their true selves and their reputation and life will be ruined. The narcissist generally will choose the person who is the most dependent on the narcissist financially, emotionally, or in any form, in order to be able to have an effect on the person and ruin or damage their life, psyche, mental state of mind etc. They will often choose the person closest to them in some form, though abuse can happen by many different people in many different forms and the chosen target isnt always someone the abuser knows very well or is close to.

You were not chosen by the narcissist or other abusers because you are weak, prone to abuse or because something is wrong with you. You were chosen because these are disordered sick people and predators and they had an opportunity to victimize you in some form, due to usually circumstances, opportunity, timing, and the involvement of other abusers past or present. Yes, once you are traumatized and victimized, your boundaries will be destroyed and even if you still have healthy boundaries, your energy will be of a certain type- full of unresolved emotions and trauma that others especially predators pick up on.

You might be quieter, unsure of yourself, be a people pleaser, apologize a lot, be extra nice, act as if deep down you feel the need to prove yourself to others, feel as if something is wrong with you, and narcissists and other predators will pick up on that. The abuser or others are not above you, but as the victim, you will tend to feel beneath others depending on the level of abuse that has been done to you. You will feel as if you really can't belong because of what has happened or what is happening to you.

This is one of the sick isolation techniques used by the disordered narcissist and abuser in order to isolate you from others and make sure you are constantly feeling inferior and suffering internally. To be destroyed by a creature that is psychopathic in nature is very frightening and the mere association with this person can be difficult to handle somewhere deep within as well.

Narcissists often target those close to them

The narcissists will often target their supposed significant other (who usually can't even qualify as a significant other due to the type of abuse being done to that person), a close family member such as a child, or parent, or a close friend, and often co-workers or others who they feel might be affected by the abuse, who can't get away from the narcissist and who they can get away with abusing who might not be able to speak up for themselves or who might not be able to defend themselves against their abuse.

They might choose meek, humble, quiet people or people who are people pleasers, kind, caring, compassionate people. People with humility, integrity who might be shocked by the behavior and be unable to respond or react or deal with it, or just really nice people who might let the abuse slide due to their kind nature. They often tend to choose empathic people, or people of a good nature or those who would be most affected by the abuse, and would be damaged the most. They may target someone who doesn't have a large support system or many friends, because they would make an easy target and would be unable to get help from the abuse or wouldn't have anyone to turn to for help.

Narcissists would ruin their social circle and life if they targeted others

If the narcissist attempted abusing their good friend, well the friend would just be shocked and probably cut off contact with them and of course, they would lose their supply of narcissistic supply, which is just a person they're using to gain admiration from, adoration and other things. They would expose their inner selves to this person, and they wouldn't be able to handle that, and that person might in turn spread rumors about them or tell others how evil they are and others would believe them. They would risk losing their false identity of being a true, moral and upstanding citizen to others, and their life would be a greater wreck than it already is.

They would also lose their social circle which a narcissist generally has. The narcissist can't risk doing anything of this nature, so they resort to abusing very specific people in their circle of friends or family, or others, those who they can abuse or target secretly, who wouldn't be able to find help for the abuse, and they make it all worse by smearing the victim's character or actions to their family and friends often slandering them in harsh ways making up lies and stories.

They make sure to isolate the victims in all kinds of ways, so that the victim is left shocked, traumatized and confused by everything the narcissist is doing to them, and then the narcissist will gain happiness and glory from their abuse, continue to seem to be happy and make more and more friends increasing their circle of friends, while the victim's circle of friends is non-existent or dwindling until there is only the narcissist left.

Narcissists would be exposed if they targeted others, so they choose people close to them

The narcissist will often target a partner, close friend or family member and rarely others because they wouldn't be able to have an effect on others, and even need to keep their abuse and malignant side as secretive as possible.

They also use others against the victim in open smear campaigns, extreme slander, and as a false reminder that there is something wrong with the victim, and to flaunt to the victim that there is something wrong with them, and often they will bring those other peoples self-esteems up, be very positive towards them, and even give the energy and happiness of the narcissist which they stole to those others. The narcissist is always using other people against the victim whether they announce it or not.

Others will be treated with extreme respect by the narcissist abuser while they will make angry sour faces at the victim and lash out at them angrily often and do the most heinous disturbing abuse to them including gaslighting, minimizing, denial and anything in their power which they can use against a person.

Narcissists use everyone they can to hurt, or destroy a victim

They will often use other narcissists against the victim and if a victim has been targeted by a different abuser rather than helping the victim out, they might justify some of the other abusers' actions validate them in some form, or even attack the victim further or in horrendous ways in order to do more damage to the victim and to damage their self-esteem and power.

The narcissist takes any opportunity they can to further demean and victimize the victim and not let them regain their power or sense of control, especially other abusers or narcissists. They are openly predators and as they age, they get worse and seem to have less care for their behaviors. They have no real shame and feel no guilt or remorse for any of their actions and will never take responsibility for them, only make them worse and project them onto their victims, and even blame the victims for their own actions.

The narcissist will often use this form of dangerous triangulation against a victim to further ruin their self-worth, even if it has been done numerous times and especially while they are devaluing the person. If they are in a phase of being nice to a victim, they will continue to use different tactics against them or abuse them depending on the scenario, but then go back to being nice to them or whatever they feel they can get away with at the time or what the victim might handle or allow.

If a narcissist usually goes all out on a victim, they are in desperate need to gain control of a victim or are going through a difficult time themselves, and will project their inner turmoil onto the victims callously.

The narcissist does target people who aren't close to them as well, but this isn't the case as often. Those who target random people or others are usually sociopaths or psychopaths or more people put in that category. Though most narcissists are psychopaths or sociopaths their abuse patterns and behavior may vary and differ slightly. They often target those nearest and dearest to them as opposed to just random people.

Victims must endure extreme amounts of torment and trauma

The victim is generally destroyed in all kinds of various horrifying ways and after enduring extreme trauma, torment, and torture at the hands of the sadistic and mentally ill, full of rage narcissist, will try with great difficulty to crawl out of the hole the narcissist has put them in, and attempt to repair the major damage done by this person. The narcissist will have none of that, as they will fight themselves to make sure that their victims aren't only destroyed, but are done so in so many creative and horrifying ways that it's close to impossible for them to recover, heal themselves, or even get away. They very carefully disarm their victims' boundaries, sense of self-worth and shatter their very core and soul. Even after destroying their victims in many creative, extreme, terrifying ways, sometimes hundreds or more, the narcissist simply will not stop.

If a narcissist chose you as victim, it only means they saw an opportunity to victimize someone in some form and thought they would be successful in doing so in gaining what they want from them, and doing so without any real consequences. They usually choose victims in an opportunistic nature, as well as people who might have great qualities that they can steal or destroy and gain the most destruction to and reactions from. Sometimes they do choose people as well who may have issues, problems or those who they perceive as weaker, broken, who've been through other forms of abuse already, or who can easily be manipulated.

Everyone is an easy target for the narcissist, as the nature of their abuse is so vicious and destructive, it can affect anyone from the strongest people and those who've never encountered any form of abuse, to those who may be perceived as weak by the narcissist- other damaged people with issues or problems of their own- not that those with issues or problems are weak people by any means, but many times predators will target those who've already been victimized because their boundaries have been destroyed in some way and they have a harder time fighting the abuse or being able to escape it, or are simply too weak internally to be able to handle more of it.

They take every opportunity they can find to choose the right targets, yet they can't target everyone or many depending on the nature of their own disorder, due to the fact that most of them want to present a facade of perfection to others and to themselves in some way and so they can show others they are moral decent upstanding good humans and citizens, not abusive malignant monsters who hurt others.

They also wouldn't be able to get away with targeting or hurting others because those others don't really care about them or are close to them and this is why they choose only people who are close to them usually because it's their only opportunity or chance at this and because it's something that they began with years ago, and have been doing so for a very long time and they've become accustomed to the abuse, power, and control or may even have a need for it.

Chapter 6

Narcissism and Evil

Narcissists are inherently evil predators

Narcissists are definitely evil creations and commit anything that isn't beneficial or helpful to others, especially to their victims.

The idea of evil is subjective and can take on different meanings depending on cultural, religious and philosophical beliefs. In general, evil refers to morally reprehensible or harmful actions, behaviors or intentions that violate ethical and moral norms.

Evil can be exhibited in different forms such as acts of violence, cruelty, exploitation, oppression and injustice. It can be perpetrated by individuals or groups who seek to exert power, control, or domination over others. It is tied to moral and ethical values, which are shaped by personal, cultural and social norms and beliefs. Some feel that evil is an inherent part of human nature, while others believe that it is a result of outside influences, such as societal or environmental factors. The definition of evil seems to be complex, subjective and open to interpretation.

Narcissists are your typical abusers- they aren't going around mistreating and hurting others, only specific targets. They are very well in control of their actions and do not need to do the ill acts they commit upon these targets. They are very evil because they choose to behave in this manner and pattern towards these people, and then throw the blame all onto them.

Abusers choose to impose their behavior upon chosen targets. They aren't being forced to do this and in most cases, they don't have a deep rooted desire to behave in this form or a complete lack of control. They do lack the idea of self-awareness or introspection and although they very well know they are committing these actions, they choose to ignore them and pretend they aren't really doing them.

They also possess a mental illness along with this disorder, and lack the concept of right vs wrong and for holding accountability. Most narcissists do not have a conscience, or really have a true moral code they exist by. It is a free for all on their victims, and towards their victims is when their moral code often becomes shattered, and they will impulsively behave in indecent or evil ways. This is because they lacked proper development sometime in their childhood or as they were growing up, and learned specific behaviors and techniques from those around them and these behaviors became ingrained within them.

Many narcissists have developed into sociopaths and psychopaths and most that are narcissists have these traits as well- they are simply not doting, self-aggrandizing, arrogant individuals who have developed a personality disorder only- they exhibit a lack of empathy and an impulsivity to do evil or harm to others, and extreme damage and destruction to people's lives.

Many commit other criminal acts such as theft, fraud, forgery, financial crimes, or all kinds of crimes that may exist out there not only towards their victims but in general, though it is often done through as hidden of means as possible since the narcissist doesn't want to face getting caught or exposed. Their disorder is a very complicated mix of unhealthy narcissistic behaviors, extreme abuse, psychopathic and sociopathic behaviors combined with a disordered personality and a lack of accountability for any actions committed.

Narcissists are very dangerous predators and many of them are very capable of murder and various crimes, and most narcissists have and will commit criminal behaviors without any sense of remorse or guilt. Narcissistic personality disorder isn't just a personality disorder whereas a person has an inflated ego and an elevated sense of self or importance- they will commit atrocious acts towards others, usually their victims, while remaining upstanding enough citizens to the outside world or to those who aren't their victims. These particular people lack empathy for others and a working conscience.

They are capable of a large number of evils, and they often hold no limits or bounds to the atrocities they are capable of committing. They will often have fooled those around them since they present themselves to be extremely kind, caring or compassionate, normal people and will be extremely nice and positive to friends, family, or those whom they haven't held hostage in their sick narcissistic psychopathic world of pathology- and theirs is an intricate world of pathology.

They are not normal people or beings, they are extremely hostile and pathological creatures, that can even be compared to zombies in nature. The nature of abuse they commit upon others isn't just a one time or hundred-time scenario- they will do extreme amounts of irreparable damage to a victim, and they really will not stop the extreme harshness of their abuse, it will continue so long as a victim is around and present and somewhere in the narcissist's life or presence.

Yet, even if a victim is able to get away from the narcissist and create a life without them or discard them from their own life, the narcissist will still find ways to destroy a victim if they desire to do so, and may attempt to hurt a person's life even if they have cut ties with the narcissist.

Abusers who commit evil actions are similar to any other psychopath or sociopath who does evil deeds. They may not be completely evil and have good in them too. They are usually not all evil, though doing these evil deeds and even criminal reprehensible acts and destruction of other peoples lives makes them very evil people in nature though they generally will do good to others.

Many narcissists commit criminal acts

Every narcissist I have encountered or dealt with has committed many forms of criminal acts or behaviors from theft, fraud, forgery, to even more wicked acts and some narcissists are full-blown sociopaths who mostly exhibit these kinds of behaviors. There are some who commit criminal actions only against their victims in some form or in their lives, yet the sheer kind of evil they are capable of can be shocking. They are very evil in nature and within and hold no form of conscience, accountability, and often just deny and blame it on their victims all while attempting to hold a false persona of being a Godly, or upstanding citizen of the world, a great parent, a good son or daughter, yet behind the façade is a very disturbed creation.

Deep down, they are often proud of the heinous acts they commit against suspecting innocent people, and internally gloat over these deeds or actions while outwardly getting angry and upset that they were accused of these things, claim they never happened, it was the fault of the victimized, or the victim is just making things up and committed the actions themselves. Sometimes, they even outwardly gloat over the manner in which they are behaving or the evils they have done, but that is just to show their true inner selves, and to even shock the victim.

They are pathological liars who will make up any given story to defend their treacherous acts upon a person, and to make sure they are constantly shedding any immoral act they commit off themselves in any way, shape or form possible. Normal people have healthy boundaries, and may even vent in healthy ways if they have to. Narcissists will remove the blame from them in any way they can and lying is one of the few ways they remove any responsibility for their own selves, often projecting it onto others, mostly their victims.

Projection is the act by which they just shed their evil, indecent or wicked acts upon others, so they don't have to internalize them or feel guilty for doing them, and just pretend they are gone and aren't happening or didn't happen. It Is a disordered, mentally sick and primitive, evil way of attempting to handle anything they have done which the victim might disapprove of or be harmed by and attempt to confront them with.

Narcissists never learned how to conceptualize their own behaviors, or understand what they are doing and how it relates to theirs and other people's lives. They not only lack empathy, they lack basic internal behavioral abilities, and lack the ability to process actions and behaviors, their own feelings and lives, and were simply not shown how to identify their own actions and how to empathize with other people's feelings.

Narcissists lack self-awareness and empathy

They lack the awareness of what it's like to hurt another person or the concept of caring for how a person feels, though they will show you otherwise. They will show an extremely caring empathetic person who might care about animals in some form, people, children. They may even give gifts to relatives and others like a normal person would- however deep down they lack self-actualization and any form of awareness.

They lack self-analysis and have no clue who they really are or what they are feeling and why. Many times, they can often be hypersensitive to things or other people's actions, showing the false persona that they are extremely compassionate or understand the plight of others.

One narcissist I knew was always worrying about their victim, and talked about how much they worried about them and how much they cared for them. In the meantime, they had destroyed the person's life doing not only maximum damage in the most vicious ways possible, but ensuring that the victim just could not recover for life. This is typical narcissistic behavior, as normal healthy people do not sit around worrying or fantasizing about people, especially all the time. Now worrying about someone could be alright if the person wasn't a narcissist who lashed out at the very person they claimed to care about in such extreme ways, yet it's still not a normal or healthy thing to do.

The narcissist got used to playing this caring mother role and even in old age did not find it abnormal, despite their child being a grandmother's age. Another narcissist used to sit around fantasizing about their victim, and talked about how much it had feelings for them, all while narcissistically injuring them all the time, attacking and maligning them and much more.

Many narcissists will often use the "I love you so much" ploy in order to fool and confuse their victims, that they may care about them in some form, or even a lot. However, this is just a sadistic mental tactic the narcissist uses to brainwash the victim into believing all these things, so the victim can believe the lies, put their guard down and feel and think in their already abused mind that the narcissist has no ill will towards them or isn't capable of committing any harm towards them.

The Narcissist as predator

The narcissist is amongst the harshest of predators demeaning, devaluing, abusing and mistreating victims with the notion of wanting to turn the victims into their very disordered damaged selves, and constantly projecting their own hate and self-loathing onto these people sometimes accomplishing what they set out to do to them.

The narcissist demeans, and abuses the victim then devalues them for being the victim and intertwined with the narcissist, judges their life and interactions harshly, and then decides to punish them for being intertwined with the narcissist and for being a weak target of this predator. They will destroy their targets and then punish them further, for being the weak and destroyed creatures they have become.

They will create this negative song and dance with the abuse victim and then further demean and devalue the person by rendering them 'worthless', lesser than the narcissist and someone who is deserving of this abuse and inferior in some form. Typically, the narcissist doesn't originally view the victim as weak, beneath, or inferior to the narcissist, they will deep down feel a connection to this victim, and even potentially view or have viewed this person as a soulmate in some form, and if it's a family member something similar.

The narcissist will break a victim down so that the person becomes extremely weak, and unable to cope or function, and may feel they need the narcissist in some form whether emotionally, mentally, physically. they turn people into vulnerable weak people, and then will punish them for being weak and for the narcissist feels is dependency they have on them.

The narcissist is often a frightening disordered rage-infested parasite that is extremely dangerous to anyone out there, especially it's prey, and that does the ultimate forms of damage to its victims. you can compare this person to a shark, or an alligator in nature, a natural predator yet those creatures don't possess an abnormality or mental illness- they are just true to their nature and the kinds of animals they were meant to be, but a narcissist is different. they are an extremely disturbed parasite and not the kind of person you'll want any kind of encounter or relationship with.

Chapter 7

THE SPIRITUAL NATURE OF NARCISSISTIC ABUSE

In many narcissistic abuse situations, there is a higher and other spiritual component at hand often. There is usually an element of negative energy associated with a narcissist's abuse. A victim is often involved in very bad energies going on between them and the narcissist.

The Narcissist is an energy vampire

What is an energy vampire? An energy vampire is someone who drains the energy or life-force of its victim. Energetic exchanges generally take place however they aren't measured or acknowledged by people in general. Few people have the knowledge that an energetic exchange is taking place between people.

Every victim of a narcissist has the same viewpoint of their situation- they can sense a strong element of negativity, bad energy and negative disturbances that are around the narcissist. The silent treatments are often wrought with extreme amounts of negative energy. If the narcissist in my life struck, other negative elements happened to me along with this until the narcissist was somehow normal towards me again.

There are many spiritual elements involved with narcissistic behavior or abuse. Many feel the narcissist was involved in a person's past life and somehow has brought those same experiences and unresolved experiences into this life and will replay the same dramas. Others feel as if extreme chaos ensues and out of the ordinary negativity that a person is unable to handle or cope with.

Narcissists are beacons of dark energy. These people are not of the light. Their very essence of made up of extremely dark painful and dangerous energy. I had experienced another narcissist who was just a dark vessel of extreme darkness, and he began to steal my light too. Narcissists are extremely dark energy vampires and will often steal their victim's good energy. This person was vicious and unrelentless.

I recently had several narcissists giving me the silent treatment and they were both stealing my energy while doing so. Both purposely took my energy and there was a definite negative energy source that seemed to be involved. All narcissistic abuse is full of extremely toxic dangerous energy that is designed to really destroy a healthy normal person's make up, and to steal their positive energy.

Narcissists have developed into natural energy vampires and harbor a natural darkness within them, something that has developed within them and their own disordered selves. They are wrought with negative and dark energies that are full of a host of very toxic emotions and thoughts and experiences that have been suppressed by them.

You'll often find that narcissists rarely vent to family or friends in their life about their problems, and if they have it doesn't solve their issues or gives them a way to be able to mentally cope with or deal with those issues, so they will resort to the misery that makes up the narcissist just turn into a battery of charged unresolved emotions that are usually dark in nature.

Energetic interactions with a narcissist

Energetic interactions between a narcissist are extremely important because it's important to understand the concept that the abuser is actually stealing your power or energy and keeping it for themselves, taking it away from you and worse off, they are using it to empower others by giving it to others. Most people don't understand the concept of energetic interactions. They aren't sure what it means to steal someone's power and too often just feel as if they have become weakened and narcissist or abuser seems to have become empowered or gained power.

The narcissist or abuser gains power in many different forms. They do so by demeaning and belittling the person, through personal attacks, character attacks, mentally and emotionally this way, through the soul, and also by throwing their own negativity and negative energy onto a victim, and worse by doing these very actions they are in fact stealing a person's energy and life force, and damaging and ruining the soul.

The narcissist or abuser often will be very positive to others. Energy usually works in healthy interactions where there is give and take, or where there is mutual interaction between people where energetic exchanges are taking place in a healthy way and not through dominance or power.

Energetic interactions with the narcissist comprise of extreme amounts of hostility, rage, and hate so that they can effectively steal the energy of the target victim. It's one way of taking energy. There are also potential spiritual components at hand and other forces working with the narcissist and causing immense discord for the victim.

There may be malicious forces that feed off this negativity these interactions and who don't want the victim to progress due to their feeding off these lower vibrations. Narcissists often hold a victim's power and energy and will give it to others so that others can benefit from the victims energy not the victim. The victim is usually depleted, drained and in a state of suffering and being unable to cope live life or progress. The narcissist is everybody's friend and their victims worst enemy and destroyer.

A narcissist uses various covert disturbing tactics to steal a victim's energy

When a narcissist begins raging at a person or attacking them, they are stealing a person's energy and they know that usually- which is why they continue to do it. A person's energy becomes stolen at this very act, and the narcissist will naturally just take it for themselves using their many evil and vile tactics and for many victims, it will almost seem as if a dark force is there in the interaction or present within the narcissist.

This person will seem like some kind of strange monster in many ways. A narcissist will steal a person's power and energy in many other ways through every abusive action they commit against the person. Pretty soon, the narcissist will hold the person's power and energy and the person themselves will be unable to cope or even function, and will feel weaker and weaker, while the narcissist seems to have gained some strength from the interaction.

You'll even notice your energy on the narcissist and how they use it to gain their own personal power for themselves, and they will purposely be very positive to others. The narcissist also gains power by verbally attacking or putting someone down and just making them weaker, and in turn they feel powerful from doing this, or get a high or get elated from it. The victim will be depleted of their own energy and strength, there will be extreme amounts of painful energy full of negativity and darkness there, and there will be many trauma bonds full of traumatic energy created due to the dysfunctional abuse and bad energy the narcissist will project onto a victim.

The narcissist uses a victim's power or energy to empower others

That's so they can effectively destroy you, maintain their false perfect sense of self to others, and so they can flaunt and show to you how nice they are to others, while they mistreat you. The narcissist brings everyone else up, values everyone else, and devalues the victim.

They will also be nice to others to flaunt all the positive energy they hold of yours and show you how they are empowering others using your very energy and power. The narcissist holds a victim's energy and power and gives it away to everyone else. The narcissist is rarely destroying other people's lives- they are usually helping others out or trying to be positive to them. That's because they want to destroy the victim only, and do heinous things to the victim and make them suffer in any way they can including giving their energy away to others, which is noticeable to the victim sometimes.

The narcissist wants to make sure their victims are down in the dumps long-term and that the victim's power and energy are being used to give good energy and positivity to those around them, while the victim is weak and in desperate need of that positivity power or energy. The narcissist will rarely be positive to the victim maybe sometimes, depending on the given situation. They will never give the victim their power back but will give the victim's life force, soul and power everything they have stolen, to everyone else to further empower them, and carefully make sure they aren't damaged or hurt and that they are happy, healthy people living good lives.

Narcissists and Empaths

An empath is a person who has the ability to feel and understand other people's emotions and experiences as if they were their own. Empaths are very sensitive to the feelings of others and can often sense their emotional state without being told. This can be both a blessing and a curse, as it can be emotionally draining to constantly absorb the emotions of others.

The narcissist hates the empath. This disordered creature feels this way simply because the empath tends to be very good in nature generally, while the narcissist possesses the traits of being extremely selfish, wicked, evil, and has traits of sociopathy and psychopathy present within them. People with these kinds of traits or personality disorders are usually going to not like a person who is of high, good and pure energy and who is of the light. As a high energy empath, I have been heavily involved in many energetic interactions with a narcissist, all against my will, for which the outcome consisted of the narcissist constantly trying to steal my energy and usually resorting to a variety of creative and disturbing tactics.

There are dark empaths out there but many empaths are of the light and these are the ones who this narcissist tends to take advantage of through different means. Narcissists lack empathy in a huge way. They lack the ability to put themselves in other people's shoes and feel for them, though there are narcissists that do feign or seem to have feelings for people, places, or object in all kinds of ways, though it's questionable whether those feelings are genuine. There are parts of this disordered individual that can feel or seem to express reactions or sympathy towards other creations in one form or another.

Narcissists generally target a few victims, like most abusers, however, every person out there is used by the narcissist in one form or another to destroy the victims of this predator. The empath is typically a kind, caring individual with high energy, who has a good amount of kindness and caring in themselves, and who has good intentions for others. The narcissist feels differently- the empath has happiness and good energy- something the lower energy narcissist does not have.

They are extremely envious of this person, the empath for possessing these traits that the narcissist simply cannot possess. The narcissist will especially choose this kind of victim, so they can destroy and denigrate them and steal more from their soul as opposed to someone who doesn't have these kinds of qualities.

Deep down the narcissist hates the empath and seeks to steal their energy because the empath's energy allows the narcissist some way of being able to deal with the toxic mess that rages within and around them. They also want to make sure to turn their empath victim into a mess of dark emotions and turn them into themselves and even if the empath is unconsciously giving them energy they will go to great lengths to steal it all so they can gain the glory the empath possesses and have, all the happiness they've gained while turning the victim dark and bitter like them and even trying to steal their happiness altogether.

They, emblems of evil and bitterness, despise the goodness that empaths possess and in turn, hate their good energy even though it heals them. They just seek to destroy the empath because of their innate goodness, and positive spirit and healing energy. They still steal their energy, use it for themselves, give it to others, and drain and ruin them in any way possible. They even punish the empath for having the ability to help or heal them.

The narcissist is extremely jealous of the empath because the empath has a great number of positive and good qualities and everything the narcissist just doesn't possess or once had before they were taken over by their disorder. They will do anything in their power to destroy the empath and at first will feed off them like a parasite feeds off a host.

Narcissists and dark empathy

Narcissists often possess dark empathy- dark empaths are simply predators who are able to use energetic exchanges and energy against someone rather than harvesting positive energy to use to heal or benefit one another. Dark empaths which is a trait many narcissists do possess, allow the narcissist to be able to understand, know and feel the emotions of others and use this knowledge to harm or hurt them, exploit them or for some form of personal gain rather than to help them or nurture them in some way.

Narcissists will somehow have the knowledge and intuitive knowing of how a person feels and may be able to understand those feelings deep within but will use their abilities or energetic abilities against someone rather than being of benefit to them. Many narcissists lack internal awareness of anything and possess and glib, shallow and fake exterior and personality that is a façade they present to others.

They lack the ability to possess true introspection or knowledge of inner depth, yet many are intelligent enough to recognize this in some form and have rejected or ignored it due to the narcissistic injury it causes them and the inability to handle the darkness that they are or that is present within themselves. Many narcissists become energy vampires or have that natural tendency inside of them to steal other people's energies, bring them down and turn them into defenseless people who are unable to fend for themselves against this vicious predator.

Narcissists are adept predators and will use anything they can against a victim of theirs and any form of knowledge they have about the person, place, or object. Dark empaths use what is called cognitive empathy exclusively because they understand someone else's thoughts and feelings without getting emotionally involved. While emotional sympathy is the act of feeling someone else's emotions as if you are also experiencing them. Compassionate empathy combines both the cognitive and emotional aspects, creating an understanding of other's emotions along with a response as if you were feeling them yourself.

The Narcissist as an energy vampire

What is an energy vampire? An energy vampire is someone who drains the energy or life-force of its victim. Energetic exchanges generally take place between people, however they aren't measured or acknowledged by people in general. Few people have the knowledge that an energetic exchange is taking place between people. Narcissists however are extremely dangerous and destructive energy vampires who usually have a strong sense and knowledge of the energetic exchanges going on between they and their victims and know exactly how to steal a person's energy in the most damaging form possible.

Energy is very real, and energetic interactions occur continuously between people, it's just that most people don't recognize what is going on, or if they do, they often ignore it and it's not usually talked about or discussed.

Now, there are narcissists who are real and true energy vampires, who have the knowledge of energetic manipulation and will actually steal energy through this means, though it might be more difficult to find or meet ones of this nature, though they do exist. I have encountered several of this kind of real energy vampire and they are of course the most dangerous to exist and ones you must get away from right away. Metaphysical energy vampires will steal the positive energy of their victims and dump negative energy onto them. Most narcissists are just natural and very adept energy vampires and will begin to feed off their target the way a parasite feeds off a host, except a narcissist is in fact far more destructive than your average parasite.

The narcissist is the most vitriol and toxic of energy vampires to exist. They exist solely as beacons of destruction to an unsuspecting or even suspecting victim of theirs. If hanging out around you and knocking things over will give you energy of any sorts, they will never do it, but if doing that steals your energy in any form, they will do it so viciously and callously, that you will not be able to recover. The narcissist is the most dangerous, destructive and toxic energy vampire to ever exist, and their goal is to make sure to steal every bit of everything you possess and take your life force, your vital important energy and drain you any and every chance they can get.

Once a narcissist begins hurting or devaluing you, they simply cannot stop. They become addicted to draining and taking from you and with a narcissist it's not even an addiction, it's just a sickness they possess in order to make sure you yourself are losing your energy, because they really don't want your energy or any part of you- they just want to steal that life force of yours so you'll become weak, an easy target and prey from them, unable to recover and so they can be above you in some form, while you are down or they are destroying you.

The narcissist is a master energy vampire, and really they aren't even masters at it- they are masters at doing the most dangerous and hostile toxic damage to you, the victim, while stealing your energy, using you as a punching bag and lashing out at you making sure your energy is a mess of their own toxic emotions, vitriol, hatred, while they project this onto you in the most callous way possible ensuring you simply won't be able to recover or gain momentum or strength, especially your own strength back.

The narcissist will purposely behave and act in very specific manners towards and around their victims and in their lives in order to steal or leech their energy in the most effective ways possible in order to steal their self-worth, esteem, and general life-force so that the victim is just an empty shell, sort of like what the narcissist truly is inside.

The narcissist isn't empty inside anymore enough, since they are stealing other people's energy, especially that which is of their victim. This is also one of the sole reasons they may choose these specific people as victims, especially high-energy empaths so they can steal their energy and use the good they have within for their own broken, distorted, twisted selves. They will then harness the victim's energy as their own cultivating it within their own self and energy body, jealous of the fact that that person possesses that energy that actually makes them feel so good, while the narcissist really has no real energy of their own most of the time or it has become so dark and damaged due to their very dysfunctional and evil natures.

The narcissist isn't empty any longer as they will continue the cycle of stealing the good energy from the victim and many times the victim of the narcissist may have no clue this exchange is even taking place. They still however, remain empty dysfunctional vessels overall, for this part about them will never change- they will remain the disordered creatures they are- unhappy, living in misery, self-loathesome, angry and bitter inside, despite stealing the life force or energy of others and using it as their own.

The narcissist is a low energy creation- maybe they did have good energy a long time back, but that all changed as life moved forward. The narcissist lost their true and primary source of energy and then began using others, especially its victim for energy or unsuspecting others. Most narcissists do have low energy and will steal it from their victims. Others have high energy, yet still have no idea how to process this energy, and will still steal from their victims ensuring the need to bring them down and leave them weak and dependent in some form.

The narcissist as a predatory metaphysical energy manipulator

The energy vampire's narcissistic abuse is comprised of the regular abuse tactics that a narcissist will use against an unsuspecting victim, and on top of this heinous mistreatment, you will find the most dangerous energetic component involved as well. The energy vampire's abuse is a dangerous predatory narcissist using energy to carry out all kinds of abuse tactics such as projective identification, projection, raging, and making a victim suffer in many forms. Energy vampire narcissists will use energy that contains feelings and intentionally project it onto the victim in frightening, rage-filled, disordered ways.

Anyone who is perceptive to energy will notice this interaction occurring, and they do it for that very reason- to project those exact feelings onto the victim, so the victim can in turn then feel exactly what the narcissist is feeling. Rather than harassing or yelling at the victim, they will use energy to force the victim to feel how they are feeling internally and do so on purpose as a very scary, dysfunctional, unnecessary and painful energetic interaction. It's a sick energetic form of projective identification. The energy narcissist knows exactly what they are doing and does so with precision.

I have dealt with a number of energy vampires of this nature. They were not fun or interesting interactions, and having to encounter this form of predator is extremely destructive and painful. They are not only a narcissist, coupled with a damaging dangerous destructive energy vampire, they are often dominant in sociopathic traits and are criminal in nature. Most of these types of predators will usually strike a victim for a long period of time, and the victim often cannot stop the abuse or painful energetic interactions.

One narcissist energy vampire I dealt with explained to me through a website he created how he could manipulate how I felt, made me feel how he wanted me to feel, and showed me how he projected emotions, feelings and energy onto me based on what he wanted me to feel or what he was feeling. Energy vampires of this nature might actually feed off a person for a long time and not stop. They usually create a mechanism by which they feed off a person, stealing their energy, life force or positive energy, and dumping negative energy back into their aura or energy body.

The narcissist seeks to steal a victim's light and goodness

The narcissist also becomes addicted to doing evil actions towards their victims, and from stealing their energy and using it for themselves. The Narcissist isn't just vested in stealing the targets major energy source and life force and using it for themselves, something they do callously, and become very addicted to due to their own lack of energetic development and lack of internal energy within or damaged energy, but they are heavily vested in making sure the victim stays weak and unable to fend for themselves in this scenario and loses their life force completely, and this is just another element of abuse the narcissist uses to steal from their targets and make sure the targets become helpless prey, rather than the strong thinking independent individuals they used to be.

The narcissist is just an empty vessel of nothingness except disordered displaced emotions, bad negative energies, and repressed emotions and feelings that they have no clue what to do with or how to deal with, so it's become part of their general dysfunctional frightening aura and inner self.

Anything the narcissist does which involves energetic vampirism, or any form of abuse that they commit towards their victims is full of chaotic rage, hate, and extreme disordered hostility in many forms. Narcissists lack the true intellect to be able to even carry out their abuse with any form of precision or real effectiveness so they tend to resort to copious amounts of extreme hostility and disordered abuse which results in the victim becoming bombarded and engulfed in the most disordered way with pain, rage, hatred, animosity and vitriol, negative energy, by the abuser, which causes extreme disarming of one's inner self and life force.

The narcissist will simply just throw the biggest rage-filled tantrum like a child towards their victims and this tantrum will never end. Even after the tantrum of rage-filled abuse, their abuse just will not end. The narcissist has to ensure that their victim has lost their soul, their inner energy source, and that they really won't be able to recover or cope with the situation at hand.

The narcissist seeks to steal every bit of good, light and energy that the victim possesses, leaving them with no energy, and the narcissist will continue stealing their soul and energy even after they have taken it all.

They want to make sure the destroyed victim is unable to recover from the abuse and once they do, they can never fully regain the strength they had prior, and that they will be a more crumbled lesser form of self that the person once was before they were bombarded with the narcissist's hate filled destructive abuse and patterns. Basically, the narcissist is generally such a mentally challenged idiot all they do is rage and lash out at the victim in a plethora of horrifying creative ways ensuring the victim is going through extreme amounts of trauma and shock and unable to handle the abuse being done to them.

They do use other forms to steal energy as well including negative comments or insults, arguments, picking fights, nitpicking, asking questions in a negative way, getting in one's space, acting crazy or psychotic towards someone, or even real energetic vampirism which involves the manipulation of energy through metaphysical means, of which there are energy vampires out there that have this ability.

Contrary to what someone might think, the narcissist is not an intelligent abuser, just an out of control, haphazard maniac that has no clue what they're really doing- they simply just want the end result to occur- an extremely traumatized, damaged destroyed victim, who is now a shell of their former self or unable to regain their former self, a punching bag for this monster who will continue this cycle and pattern of abuse towards this target, who ends up turning into a shell of tragedy, scared, fearful, nervous, full of anxiety terrified victim, unable to truly function they way they used to and a person who is now a shell of a former person that doesn't exist anymore.

The narcissist has chosen this target and wants to ensure the victim will always be the target of the narcissist as long as they are around this abusive monster. The narcissist isn't always loud and boisterous- their abuse can be more secretive and they will commit a number of abuses quietly but through the most destructive means possible. Their destructive abusive isn't always abrasive in nature, for they might abuse quietly and covertly yet with extreme negativity and harshness to ruin someone's inner esteem, and other facets of themselves.

Chapter 8

Characteristics of a Narcissist

You can't confront a narcissist

If you confront a narcissist, they will easily pretend they have no clue what you're talking about, they have done nothing wrong to you and have no clue what youre talking about, they have no ill will towards you and have never done a bad or intentionally bad thing to you. You are imagining the abuse in some way. You are overemotional, over sensitive or overreacting in a huge way. They will lash out at and rage at a victim who attempts to malign their fake decent character that they believe they possess, and accuse the victim of possessing those traits, deny and project.

You have this problem with others- which you will once you've been a victim of a narcissist and that is because there are many people out there who may not be full-blown narcissists, but who may be ignorant or abusive and they will notice what they perceive as the weakness in you which will be present and what was done by the narcissist manifesting as trauma hurt or pain and they will wrongly take advantage of the weakness or hurt or pain that they feel is present within you.

They will in turn behave like predators and see you as weak, shy, submissive and attempt to dominate you in some form or feel there is something wrong with you, or know there isn't yet will still use any dark spots on you to use against you in some way and very soon you will feel like others are against you or mean or rude to you or dominating you as well. It will seem like a dominant pattern in your life unfortunately and it all stemmed from the angry vicious confused narcissist who has no clue what it's doing.

Never argue with or call out a narcissist for you will never recover from the lashing out and devaluing they will end up doing to anyone who does that. Any attempt to tell the narcissist not to something that might be harmful to you results in that narcissist lashing out at you, and causing you even more harm, all while claiming they are doing nothing wrong to you, that it's all in your head, or something of that type of sadistic toxic nature.

Narcissists lack substance or true intellect

Narcissists are not intelligent people. They are not intelligent predators, psychopaths, or skilled adept intellectuals who are deserving of any form of praise for their mental capabilities in any shape or form. They are in fact, extremely selfish and stupid morons who hold no rational form of thinking and they are extremely disordered creatures within their own selves who are lacking true intelligence.

They resort to strange and primitive behaviors that only people with brains who are lacking intelligent thought might resort to doing, and commit treacherous, dangerous acts that are generally looked down upon or possessed by psychopaths or criminals. Most abusers are not intelligent, rational people and the narcissist is generally a person who might hold a level of intelligence in some format, but the behaviors they exhibit are of an unintelligent nature, and they possess a dangerous mental illness.

They throw glibs of intellect here and there, but are usually more vested in showing their evil side and use their intellect in the pursuit of evil not good or anything that might be beneficial. Many might use their careers or benefits to do good things or help others and though it's mostly for show they may somewhere deep down have a desire to do that good, but they usually aim to destroy their targets that seems to be their primary desire over anything else. Destroying their targets often consumes their life, and their targets are usually people who are primary in their life.

They lack intellect because they are usually very evil disturbed people who are dark and angry inside, and who are taken over by their disorder which exhibits their desire to be grandiose, pathological, a liar, delusional, irrational amongst other things.

Narcissists will often use other abusers and narcissists as advantages against their targets and do so in the most vicious unjust way possible. This is a sick and deviating technique they often use called triangulation.

The narcissist uses their status or profession to victimize others

The narcissist is a pathological liar with superficial shallow and glib feelings overall towards the acts they are committing. They will never admit to any fault or wrongdoing and believe they are emblems of moral perfection while lacking any sense of their behaviors a higher awareness or any form of introspection. They will commit treasonous and treacherous acts without a second thought to the consequences of their actions and will usually act witu extremely harmful intent towards those they target or victimize.

They seek to do the most harm or damage to their victims and will often do so by lashing out at them in various harmful ways or even destroying their lives in the most effective ways possible. They aren't around just to abuse the victim and bring them down or affect their life negatively, they are there to create havoc and cause the maximum amount of damage possible.

You will often find narcissists behaving in moral and upstanding ways throughout their life while covertly destroying others or other people's lives. They may be priests preachers or people who act as if they are close to God.

Doctors, nurses, and all sorts of people of upstanding professions will be narcissists as well. Many narcissists will choose higher professions for different reasons- in order to gain power or control over others, or to put themselves in a position of nobility or superiority and often times will use their job status to flaunt their superiority over their victims or to prove their superiority in some form. The narcissist also does need those people as friends and doting followers and usually needs a large support system i.e. the support system they will not allow the victims to gain due to their extreme mistreatment and long term patterns of damaging abuse which are difficult to escape or heal from.

They need this to validate their fragile sense of self-worth and sense of self while they further destroy the victim. They want to have everything while they make sure the victim has nothing.

It gives them their place in life to be able to commit the very acts they do and gives them the real life stability and backing of being moral and noble and incapable of wrongdoing and they can always use their professions as symbols to prove their lack of possessing any bad in them, masking or hiding their evils, and proof that they are there to help others and do good deeds rather than the accusations that will often be brought out on them by those victimized by them of being evil, a monster, abusive, sick etc.

Narcissists will use any and everything they can against their victims and for their own selves and to justify their behavior which they will staunchly pretend isn't happening. They will often make their victims out to look crazy or bad and will usually have repressed their victim's own professions or personal lives so that the victim may never gain the mental power they need to back their own sense of selves up and feel empowered against these predators.

They will always hold their other or false self as a symbol of some form of perfection or moral upstanding, not committing any evil acts, yet most often the acts they have done to their victims are full of immorality and even may be criminal in nature.

The narcissist feels they are superior to others and unable to do any kind of evils or wrong. They think they are above others and above committing crimes of any kind of even mistakes. Yet ironically, their reality is wrought with criminal behavior of some sort and making mistakes all the time.

The narcissist will have turned their victim into such a toxic punching bag that they will perform their evil vicious acts against the victim in an automatic way with others turning away, ignoring the situation, or not even noticing or recognizing it. They will often just callously abuse denigrate and insult the victim or mistreat them in such outrageous ways further adding to the injuries already present, to ensure the victim just can't hold their own ground or be able to psychologically escape or cope with the abuse.

The narcissist will shatter a person's defenses, abuse, continuously destroying their boundaries, and litter their soul with hatred lascivious attacks and negativity and attack them in such a vicious and negative way and continue this behavior. Emotional abuse is second nature to this monster, and it doesn't give the victim a way to defend themselves or even be able to escape the abuse or have a method for healing or undoing the damage this predator is doing to the victim.

The narcissist will feel they are above committing criminal actions of any kind even if they have done so. Not only will they claim the actions never occurred, they will deny responsibility for any actions they have done, deny they did any of those things to a victim and they will often or always blame the victim for the actions committed or twist the situation around and say it was beneficial or necessary for the victim and even say the victim caused the actions themselves to occur.

Narcissists are sadists, and pathological liars

Narcissists want their victims to suffer. They are very sadistic in nature. These are not nice, kind decent people. They will never behave this way towards others though, because there are huge repercussions involved if they do. Though, even if they expose themselves, most people are so enamored by them, despite the fact that most of them lack any form of charm or charisma, and are very obviously mentally ill people or people with some extreme form of dysfunction.

If a narcissist is suffering, which they usually are, they will go to great lengths to project their own suffering onto the victim and can make the victim feel through extreme abuse what they are feeling deep within. It's an extremely sick tactic they have the ability to perform upon unfortunate unsuspecting victims who have already been ruined by them or are still pinned as a scapegoat according to them, for them to use and abuse as they want.

To a victim, this is extremely obvious, and not only because the victim has witnessed their Frankenstein, monster, hyde personality or that's all they know of this person, but because their behavior isn't normal, even if they put on a façade, most of the time it's obviously riddled with a lack of intellect, a fake personality, a disordered idiot in many forms, and a strange character that is obviously putting on a show.

In court, unfortunately and confusingly, narcissists usually have judges, lawyers and anyone wrapped around their finger, though it's a mystery as to why. They are obviously pathological liars, speak things that make no sense, and even if they put on a façade of appearing normal, they rarely do. It is a huge mystery as to why they are perceived to be sane, intelligent and normal when they usually display otherwise.

Their fabrications and lies are usually very obvious. Their disordered self seems to come through with their irrational words and statements. They rarely appear to be normal sane functioning people. They will often cry at odd times, put on shows and make it very obvious, yet people in courtrooms seem to take their side for some reason. Any sane person would know that the narcissist is putting on a show or fabricated lie. I've witnessed lawyers admit that a narcissist is using the court system for power and control and still do nothing about it, or side with them in some way.

Narcissists seek power and control

Narcissists, like any abuser, seek power and control, but with a narcissist it's even worse. They seek extreme amounts of power and control over their victims in any form, and when it is threatened, they will take great measures to assert that power and control back over their victim in some way, and make sure their victim is seemingly beneath them and never recovers or regains their life, strength or confidence.

The narcissist's victim will often appear crazy and powerless, and they will resort to all kinds of crazy making in order to make the victim look like the one who is the issue or who has the problem and not the most damaging perpetrator and abuser.

They will seem this way to others who are bystanders, ignorants, people not dealing or who have ever dealt with the situation, and other abusers around who too may take advantage of the narcissists victim of major and toxic abuse.

Others may support or agree with the narcissist, which is not only further damaging to the victim, but causes more trauma, and chaos within the already destroyed victim, who needs positivity, love, healing and support, but will cause the healing of the victim to go backwards and create an inversion of healing, and more negativity and pain within the victim, and they are usually unable to cope with this reality that on top of all of the abuse they are suffering, which is too toxic to be able to handle anyway, others are not helping them, but supporting the narcissist or calling them crazy or names or putting them down too.

The bystanders and ignorants on the side will usually give more support and power to the narcissist, who doesn't need any, while the victim is the one in dire need of support and help. This creates a greater negative aspect and more trauma bonds and dark pain within the victim's soul and body.

Narcissists use court systems for power and control

Narcissists are a nightmare in court systems, or really anywhere their disturbing presence tends to be. They will use the court and legal system for power and control and most of the time will commit atrocious acts against their victims, often ruining lives simply for sport, or to exercise their power and control and dominance over a victim. They are skilled at making a victim appear crazy, though to a truly sane, normal person the narcissist will obviously be lying or making up stories, but others will seemingly believe their lies, and sometimes even know they're lying, yet will still take their side.

Narcissists use any chance they can to have power and control over a victim. Many narcissists will go to court because they enjoy it, want to make the victim suffer, feel it makes the victim subservient to them, and gives them power or control over the victim's life and emotions.

Many times, a narcissist will take a victim to court, because they are bored and for this very pathological disordered person, this is interesting or even fun for them. They are in control, and the victim can't do anything usually or find it difficult to even defend themselves in the given situation. The narcissist will usually destroy the victim with a barrage of mistruths, fabrications, lies and projections. They will usually project their own issues and shortcomings onto the victim chastising them in these kinds of situations or any situation. Court is a playground for the narcissist, as is any scenario or experience which gives this disordered person any sense of power or control.

A story of a malignant narcissist in court

I relative I knew of had dealt with a very malignant narcissist who got her involved in the court system. He spent months 'setting her up' as he said, and she had no idea what he was planning. Although she was still hanging out with him occasionally, he was saving all of her text messages to send to the district attorney, and resorted to abusing her in extreme ways so she would get upset and angry with him through text. He spent months never texting the victim back, and making sure it was only one way, though he would still call and talk to her and see her in person.

He was a photographer and even resorted to having a relationship with a lawyer or some women in the court offices, and posted pictures of the sexual photoshoots he did with them online, so the victim could know what was going on. He claimed a woman in the court office was his girlfriend. He kept warning the victim that they would receive something in the mail for the 'charges' but the victim didn't believe it only because she had done nothing wrong to the narcissist and didn't feel he had a way of making up lies against her. However, this is a narcissist involved and if they want to do something they will find a way and go to extreme and horrific measures to do it.

This particular narcissist finally told the victim he 'set her up' and laughed about it all. When the victim received the paper for the charges, the narcissist was still calling her and trying to talk to her, but she couldn't talk to him. He even called her and said to her "if I drop the charges will you marry me," and asked her to marry him many times. This was all in the midst of a horrible experience done by this malignant predator, who not only held no guilt or remorse for his behavior, but who had ulterior plans to do this again in the future for no reason.

That narcissist was still in the victim's life for many years and afterwards somehow got the victim to talk to him again, and injected himself in the victim's life. He remained in the victim's life a docile, nice person who had no intent of harming the victim for many years and was a friend who barely had any communication with her.

Years later, he again threatened to ruin the victim's life or go to court, blaming her for all sorts of false, irrational things that didn't occur, and worse, he admitted he was bored and just wanted to do it. The victim attempted to get a restraining order on the narcissist, but as usual, he created lies that were projections about himself, and pinned them on the victim, and a confused, ignorant, spiteful judge decided to side with the abuser, as usual.

It's almost impossible to find protection against a narcissist, or most abusers, but especially abusers and monsters of this nature, and often times the victim is further blamed and pathologized, while the most dangerous destructive predator gets away with their vicious dangerous crimes against an innocent person.

The court system is just not designed to help out victims of abusers or narcissists for some reason. It is designed to allow control seekers, and sociopaths like the narcissist to do what they want and get away with their sick, twisted actions and really do anything they want to a victim without any repercussions. This is just a win for the narcissist and is a reminder that no one is there to stop them from doing wrong to a victim, and they always continue with their abusive actions.

They get worse with age

The narcissist will often become more mentally ill with age and their abusive abnormal behaviors and thoughts will become more deeply ingrained in them, and their abnormal way of thinking will seem normal to them. Any abnormal feelings or thoughts they possess, will become rooted in their very disordered nature and they will be unable to heal or change from this even if they tried.

Most of the time, the narcissist refuses to believe they have aged or are even aging. Outwardly, using their arrogant sense of superiority they will haughtily claim that age doesn't matter, they don't feel old, they don't look or seem old, or their behavior simply won't get better. Most victims usually expect them at some point to change their ways, or their ill behaviors towards victim, but to someone's horror, they become more ingrained and set in their abusive tendencies, and their abnormal actions, and rather than changing for the better will become worse and more grotesque.

If there is an elderly narcissist in someone's life, they will ignore the fact that the person is of a younger age and that they have no business in their life- whether they're old or young of course, but that they should finally retreat and do something else or take up a hobby. The narcissist rarely budges- to them destroying a victim is their hobby and they usually don't want to stop.

I have dealt with all kinds of narcissists and there are some common traits and patterns they possess. They usually will never hold any form of responsibility for their dark, twisted behaviors and will throw the blame on the victim and even state negative things about the victim, after or while destroying them, and worse off, they will steal the good energy and life force of the victim a lot of the time, further disempowering the victim and leaving them an empty dark shell while stealing any happiness or positivity they do hold.

They often deny the abuse is happening, destroy the victims self-esteem and then blame them while doing so for the behaviors or their responses to the abuser's actions.

Most of the time, the narcissist is a very dark, negative nasty angry vicious person deep within themselves, so they want to turn that person into what they are and once they are done with their covert, or open disturbing abuse, their victim will often feel like the narcissist does internally and the narcissist will be full of the victim's positive energy and happiness.

Many of these monsters are varying types of energy vampires and once they begin their vampirism on a host, extreme damage is usually done to the victim in the most disastrous way possible. They want to leave the victim feeling dark, down and especially empty with nothing inside, and they will easily be soul suckers and steal someone's very soul from them turning them into a mess of emptiness, darkness, and nothingness that which really comprises the narcissist.

The narcissist will usually win and get away with it all

The narcissist will almost always win and "get away with it all" unless you take action against them however, even if you take action against them, they will still win. They will never truly win, because they are the malignant disordered monsters they are, but you can never defeat a predator at their own game or destroy them. Society is designed to make sure you just don't. Therapists may not help and will usually pathologize the victim or further mess with their heads through sadistic means or faulty therapy techniques.

Victims are often silenced, rarely validated in a positive way, and the narcissist will gain all the praise and validation for committing their crimes and evils from confused or even evil others or bystanders who themselves lack introspection or really don't care about the situation, could care less, and find it easier to just blame the victim too. The narcissist will always almost be enabled by others and will be shocking for the victim to witness. Yoh would think justice would or prevail but it doesn't.

You can get away, break free from the abuse, move on, gain your power or life back and you will always be the winner of course because you aren't them, but in the hell they create for you, they will always defeat you or ruin your life. That's nothing to be proud of or gloat over, of course.

You can attempt to report them for their behaviors, call the police if they committed a crime, win in court if that's involved, get revenge on them, or stand up for yourself (which isn't possible with a narcissist). If you attempt to stand up for yourself the narcissist will just ignore you and resort to more destructive abuse tactics and just make you suffer more.

Never battle a narcissist in court. Of course, unsuspecting victims have no choice once they are put in any given situation like this. If you have to protect yourself then do so, but just remember it's important to discredit their lies and slander that they use against you and prove the truth and then they will back off in some way.

If you have to go to court against a narcissist they will often win using lies, slander, smear campaigns, brainwashing, and will seem to have everyone wrapped around their finger though it's obvious they are very mentally Ill. It can be shocking and confusing for any intelligent person to witness. If a narcissist knows they might lose in court, they will drop the case if it's possible, or do whatever they can to leave the situation since they hate losing and definitely don't want the victim to beat them and win.

The golden child and all their friends will be there to support the narcissist. The narcissist and all their friends will be there to support them in their abuse towards the victim. No one will be there to stand up for the victim or help them out. Everyone will pathologize the victim and support the narcissist.

They will rarely change or heal

Never expect a narcissist to admit they have committed any wrongs or even crimes against a victim, for they believe they are perfect and do no wrong and will never feel they have hurt or abused you in any way and will often project it back upon you and do even more abuse to you and claim you're abusing them and that you even deserve it in some form because you're the one picking fights with them or lashing out at them. They often throw their own behavior back at the victim and want the victim to bear the burden of abuse they're doing to them plus the notion that the victim is the real abuser not the narcissist.

Confronting a narcissist will result in a few things- the narcissist ignoring your confrontation or accusations, the narcissist denying it all and throwing it back on you, or the narcissist reacting with intense and extreme rage towards you, further abusing you more to somehow twistedly prove their actions aren't wrong or evil- they will try to prove they're justified in this very sick behavior and act upon it even harder and with more wrath. They also want to prove they are perfect and that you have no right or place to ever accuse them of anything they have actually done or accuse them of anything period.

That's to prove to you they are perfect no matter what and it's even more thrilling to them to damage you even further, since you weren't expecting such a backwards response to this. The response that they enjoy is the one that you will be extremely damaged and shocked by their evil extremely uncalled for behavior and they will continue with the abuse.

Narcissists are not powerful people or creatures

They are usually very inferior, scared, weak predators who are abnormal internally in ways you can't imagine. They really hold no power in any way shape or form. Usually, they hold the victim's power in some way, or the victim feels they do, and this is the only thing that makes them truly powerful. Some of them may hold great jobs or seem to be powerful people in high places, but usually the narcissist is a weak, scared dilapidated predator, who is very dangerous and behaves like a scary monster. They are however, extremely dangerous pathological predators and can do severe damage to a victim's mind, soul, emotions and life. Narcissists aren't just in it to 'abuse a victim.' They are out to ruin a victim's life and usually do so more than once.

Narcisissts know exactly how to destroy a victim

It usually seems strange that they know exactly what to do, say, or how to act and behave in order to disarm their target, trigger them and then ensue abuse sessions with them, and make them suffer. They have often been doing it for so long, so they know exactly what to say, what to do and how to push a victim's buttons, to get reactions out of them, abuse them or take their energy. Most narcissists are just negative beacons of darkness, and will automatically steal a victim's energy somehow, and have gained an innate sense of how to do this- it's part of their very make up now. Victims are usually confused and shocked at the methods the narcissist employs against them, even if they have been done hundreds of times. The narcissist seems to know every detail and idea revolving the victim and they know exactly how to ruin their day, what to say to upset them, and how to get narcissistic reactions out of them.

Chapter 9

STORIES OF NARCISSISTS

A narcissist unable to handle their life situation

A narcissist was going into surgery and couldn't handle all the various difficult elements going on in her life. Her relatives had just visited and had left, and she couldn't deal with going back to her life of old age loneliness and misery, so she decided to slowly lash out at her target a week prior to her relatives coming. She had become accustomed to lashing out at the victim and it was normal for her to do, despite being nothing but kind and caring towards everyone else. While her relatives were there, the victim made a comment to the narcissist about something they were doing to the victim, and the narcissist began doing it more to the victim and even said "you asked for it" angrily (because the victim accused the narcissist of what they were doing).

After her relatives left, she was still distraught and decided to shock the victim by lashing out at them in the middle of a restaurant outing. The victim was terrorized, confused, traumatized and asked the narcissist just to be nice to them and not to destroy this experience, yet the narcissist got angrier and worse, and began lashing out at them more, then blamed the victim for the abuse and said they wished they had a camera to show family and friends how abusive the victim was towards the narcissist.

This particular narcissist wouldn't let the victim get away with having an ounce of happiness during her surgery, or to the days leading up to it. Because her surgery was a life changing event she was unable to handle, she decided to project her fears, anger, loathing and inability to handle the situation in the most destructive way on her target, an innocent victim. The level of anger and hate she displayed towards the victim and negativity was too much to comprehend. After attempting to recover from it all- which the victim was unable to do since she was dealing with other negative and toxic frightening people who normally didn't behave this way, she was finally able to gain a little bit of positivity in the midst of everything.

The vicious narcissist had an anger towards the victim over something she had accused her of weeks prior, and had also been punishing her since for that. She constantly kept repeating the accusation- which wasn't a big deal- and said "you asked for it!!" angrily, weeks prior.

The negativity and abuse was beyond too much to even remotely fathom. The day of her surgery, the victim didn't attempt to call or ask how she was. During a facetime conversation with others the victim asked her how she was doing. During the conversation she made a really horrible blatantly nasty comment about the victim regarding the accusation that had been made about her weeks prior. She did so in the most negative way possible to malign the person's character, insult them unjustly, and treat them in some really negative sick way which least expected, since she had just come out of surgery, and was weak and not feeling well. Millions of people undergo surgery. People don't lash out at others or take their fears and frustrations out on others.

For the victim, it was something too brutal to describe. After so much abuse, negativity, and pain the victim had to endure, she was finally starting to feel a little bit better and try to recover from it all, yet there was the narcissist again to throw it all back at her. The narcissist acted as if the accusation was made towards her was the most horrendous thing to say about someone. If it wasn't true, that would be one thing, but it was all the plain truth.

After the narcissist made those comments about the victim, the victim slowly was engulfed in some kind of strange darkness and felt her life force just leave her. She was in shock and confusion as to how that happened and came to the conclusion that narcissists are just accustomed to doing this to their victims- stealing their life force, and they almost do it naturally or automatically without thought.

The reason I bring up energy so often is because the energetic interaction between a narcissist and victim is one that is quite frightening in nature. The narcissist is slowly trying to turn the victim into them and steal their goodness, good energy and much more.

A narcissist blaming and raging at a victim for something minor

I had dealt with a passive-aggressive covert male narcissist once who began a rage campaign on me just because a male invited me somewhere. Once I told the narcissist I was invited somewhere, he began blatantly harassing and attacking me in false anger. He wasn't even angry about the situation and if he was, well he was vindicated by attacking me for it. However, this particular monster just didn't want to stop. He continued raging at me for days, throwing in as much negativity as he can. I tried to argue and reason with him and asked him not to be so negative, but he just wouldn't stop. He had found a way to take my energy and he began taking all of his inner anger out on me and purging onto me.

He was ordinarily a pretty passive nice person, and would never do this to his friends, yet he then began this rage attack against me in all sorts of ways. He began being very negative and just wanted to take my energy mostly for other personal things that weren't happening in our relationship or friendship, and for his lack of intellect, introspection, everything. He then began to take his anger out on me regularly and felt justified in doing so.

He began gaslighting me and denying text messages he wrote, and accusing me all sorts of strange things that didn't happen. He admitted he was doing it because I was 'happy I got invited somewhere,' and continued on with the rampage. At the time, he was one of my few close friends, and I felt safe enough to have him as a primary friend, though he had done something abusive to me a year prior and I did cut off contact with him, but for some reason got back together with him months later.

This particular narcissist was an incredibly dark passive-aggressive narcissist and abuser who harbored a large amount of dark energy inside of himself. I bring up energy because that was the nature of his energy, which I could sense. He then became addicted to stealing my energy and started doing so in very strange ways. He repressed all of his emotions and feelings, had a lack of all introspection, was significantly older but claimed he felt as if he was 20, and showed immature mental development in some forms.

This person began stealing my energy constantly, and just would not stop. He would get in my space constantly, wave his hands in my face, just try to be around me, and began spewing negativity at me and I was shocked that someone like him, was behaving in this way. He already had ruined things for me in the past such as an audition I had with "The Voice."

He was always an energy taker in some form, and negative or abusive, and I even cut ties with him the year prior, but with any abuser, as the victim, I forgave the previous abuse or had forgotten the details of it, and decided to rekindle a friendship with this person. During my audition day, he began asking me lots of questions about when my audition was, and kept saying "when is your audition, when is your audition" which was strange and draining. He picked a fight with me, and I was trying hard to ignore him because I was very nervous about the audition.

He ended up just ruining how I felt about it all, and I was even more nervous about it all and didn't perform the way I should have. He also constantly asked me questions or what I was doing like fifty times of anything, and it was very draining and weird. If I had a meeting he would ask me- what kind of meeting is it, where is the meeting, who's going to be there. He would continue asking many questions and though it's not as abusive, it's rude and intrusive and I asked him not to ask me this many questions about things I was doing.

He even began to destroy experiences I had with friends or family, and decided that when my family was coming, he was angry and upset and began being really negative to me and draining and saying all kinds of negative, weird things to me. He just would not stop, and I had asked him weeks prior, to stop with the negativity but he refused to.

I was in shock, because he had just taken a special trip for weeks to go visit his family and I never ruined his experience or was rude to him. He even ruined my new job training, because he was so negative towards me, and I began to have feelings of self-doubt and confusion. This particular narcissist, just would not stop. He continued his negative attacks on me and the negative energy he exuded was something so painful I can't even begin to describe.

He was doing all of these sick behaviors intentionally and he had no reason to do them. He constantly denied things he wrote through text message, twisted everything and said the infamous mindless "I was just joking" to things that weren't jokes and that were serious abuse. He minimized, denied, blamed the victim for his own actions, and worse deep down he began to use me as a punching bag for the darkness that ensued within him- an older person with a lot of hate, anger and rage inside.

He became almost addicted to these attacks on me, or as if he felt justified in doing them at all. In person, he was generally a pretty nice person but once we met again, after all of the harsh text messages, and a few phone calls, he was behaving very strangely in person and continued his cycle of being very negative to me. He began asking me 50 questions and was very rude to me at some point, and was almost yelling at me and was frustrated and kept complaining angrily. His negativity just didn't end, neither did his energetic vampirism. He kept jumping in my aura and very close to me on purpose to take as much energy as he could of mine.

I've learned from experience that when a dark, negative psychopath type person wants to bring you down and ruin you internally, they will find a way to do so, and it will be a very scary and unfortunate thing for the victim. He was also taking his anger out on me for something that happened during his trip, that he wasn't too happy about. Although I have dealt with many narcissists, most of them being very malignant, I was still shocked at the behavior of this dark narcissistic monster of a person.

He was acting very angry towards me almost as if I did something wrong to him. This made no sense to me- as he ruined my audition, ruined my job training, ruined my experience with my family by being so negative, was eroding my self-worth and making me doubt and question myself, stealing my positive energy and throwing his dark energy somewhere inside of me, and began lashing out at me angrily just because a male invited me somewhere and I was laughing, and hadn't stopped since.

He even hit me a year prior in a restaurant, out of frustration, and called it a 'love tap' and said I was overreacting. This was a very passive-aggressive individual and a very toxic dark person who didn't seem to care he was treating me this way, and as someone told me once 'those who abuse you do so, so they can hold no accountability for it'- that's why they do it. I attempted to ask him to not be negative to me weeks prior, and he just wouldn't stop.

Ever since this narcissist began his cycle of abuse or devaluation, he just didn't stop. He got worse, and worse and became more addicted and toxic and he rarely had any positive or normal behavior towards me, only negative, rude and strange behavior. This narcissist was almost nice compared to the other narcissists I had dealt with in the past, however, his behavior was beyond toxic, unable to be dealt with in any form, and unable to handle for any person.

No matter what was said to him, he remained silent, refused to acknowledge any of the behavior he was doing, denied any of it was happening and tried to minimize it all, continued with the negative or abusive behavior, and continued being as negative or rude as possible.

He often accused me of his own behavior and was exhibiting this sad form of projection. His behavior was extremely arrogant as well the manner in which he ignored my requests for him to go back to being nice to me in some way. He was behaving like an angry psychopath in a trance almost- as if he had been wronged in some way and was justified in his behavior. Really, he was taking his anger out on someone else for the issues he had with his ex-wife or for the things he had been through with her.

Many narcissists will abuse or attack a victim quite viciously, deny it ever happened, blame it all on the victim, and even appear angry at the victim if they ever meet or talk again as if they were wronged by the victim, all while the victim has been destroyed by this predator even for years or decades, with the narcissist still denying it's happening, gaslighting or victim blaming. It's quite shocking for the victim to encounter this unintelligent predator, who is angry at the victim all after ruining their day, their experience or even their life and continuing it.

A real energy vampire narcissist who was predatory right away

I was once dealing with a narcissist in a very disturbing behavior pattern and decided to go to a spiritual group meeting that was part of a popular organization- one which I had gone to before and which seemed to be somewhat of a positive experience. I was in a very sad low and having self-doubts and internal issues and was hoping to gain some insight from any discussions or people that were present. There were just a few of us there.

At some point, one of the males there began dominating me in a very strange, awful way and wouldn't let me talk or give my opinions sometimes. His behavior was very strange and a red flag for abuse or narcissism, even possibly sociopathy. I needed a positive interaction desperately as my soul couldn't handle any negativity or abuse, I was currently dealing with. I also couldn't handle being dominated or silenced and wasn't up to the negativity he was dishing out. I also ignorantly mentioned how I tend to deal with energy vampires a lot, because I thought it was a group for positivity and goodness and that the people were innately good and had good intentions for each other, or so I thought.

I thought he was just behaving like a strange energy vampire just sucking my energy from me, attempting to dominate me in some form and bring himself up. He was almost treating me as if I was a stupid female and that's the negative outcome I was getting from his behaviors and actions and conversation with me. By the time he was done with me towards the end of the discussion, he had stolen a significant amount of my energy and I was shocked and worse he asked me for a hug. I gave him my number and he immediately began sending me all kinds of strange energy, as he could manipulate energy, which is something I found out hours later.

I sensed a lot of strange energy around me as I'm perceptive to energy and was confused as to what was going on. He explained to me he sent orbs of energy to me and then began saying that he unconsciously sends bad energy to people. His dialogue was strange and by that point I could sense that he was a very disturbed individual.

There was a lot of disturbing energy coming from him full of many negative emotions and feelings. He also began talking about how he was paranoid, and that his relative had schizophrenia, so I asked him if he had paranoid schizophrenia, and he didn't respond. His verbiage was very strange, and I decided to google his name and number, and discovered he was a sexual predator who had been convicted years prior.

Of course, I was terrified by all of this and cut ties with him immediately. Now this person wasn't just a narcissist, he was a psychopath of some sorts, and a real energy vampire. Encountering him was a very frightening and traumatic experience but he exhibited many of the traits a narcissistic would. He was overtly arrogant, callous, in his toxic behavior, and decided to victimize or target someone already because they gave him some information on how they were a current or past victim of narcissists and abusers. He immediately jumped in on the opportunity to take advantage of or victimize a female at a group that he was the host of.

Chapter 10

Narcissism and Family Dynamics

The narcissist creates hostility and dysfunction within a family

Family dynamics with regards to narcissistic abuse are extremely dysfunctional in nature. A narcissist will end up creating a very dysfunctional scenario that will now become the entire family as a whole. The narcissist will select specific victims in the immediate family to play particular roles in their disturbed disordered world. Narcissists will appear to be normal to others but their internal make up isn't like normal healthy people, it is similar to abusers or psychopaths mostly.

The narcissist might be a parent, uncle, aunt, grandparent or child but often is the parent in an immediate family setting. They will groom other family members to cater to them or to follow their actions and lead and become the household leader in a sense or already were this or played this role.

Healthy family dynamics revolve around nurturing a child, or family, creating love and harmony, and allowing the natural processes of growth and learning to take place, along with allowing children and siblings to play the roles they were meant to be, not strange ideations and concepts created by a disordered selfish conscienceless adult.

Parents nurture and comfort their children and make them feel safe, loved and protected. Narcissists do the total opposite- they create confusion, hostility and disdainment within a family, and thrive on this negativity and hatred. They want their children to grow up to be disordered people just like themselves, and do not care about the outcome of their selfish actions on those who are their very offspring.

Abuse happens, but it's difficult to fathom that parents of a child do not want the best for them, and actually seek to do them harm, albeit it's a very common concept that has dominated familial dynamics throughout history. Narcissists do not want what's best for their children- they live in a fantasy or bubble world, and only care about their wants, needs and desires. Yes, a narcissist could even be caring for and doing a successful job with regards to taking care of their children, but their main desire is to cater to their own wishes and needs, which involve creating this hatred and dysfunction and disorder within their own family life, and within their children's life and world.

The narcissist does not raise or cultivate a healthy normal family. Disorder is within their very nature. The narcissist might have reasonably or unreasonably high demands for their children or for others. This person raises through disorder, chaos, and terror and refuses to allow healthy or natural dynamics to occur within their family.

They feel they are the head honcho in the family, and others are there to cater to their needs. The narcissist often demands admiration and approval of some nature by everyone around them. To a narcissist, a child isn't their own self, but an extension of the narcissistic parent.

The child isn't perceived as an independent person with their own needs, wants, and desires- they are developed or molded into being what the narcissist wants, which will be a figure that will either praise or adore the narcissist, not be important to the narcissist, or someone who will be a scapegoat or someone who the narcissist will use to devalue, denigrate, and ruin and throw their own internal aggressions and sins upon.

The narcissist has no concept of boundaries when it comes to their own families or those who they choose to victimize. They may be overly aggressive with those people, exert their opinions aggressively and claim it's the child's opinion, feel they are always right, and everyone else is 'wrong' since they perceive things as black or white usually, and they will refuse to accept their perspectives or validate their needs. The narcissist denies and destroys boundaries and makes sure the victim has no way or means of defending themselves. Children who are afflicted with this kind of confusing negative reinforcement will often grow up confused about life, have severe self-esteem issues, have a serious distrust of others, and may be re-victimized by others.

The narcissist creates dysfunctional roles within a family
The golden child and the scapegoat

The narcissist's scenario with regards to family dynamics can be a very complicated and dysfunctional one riddled with dysfunction and strange patterns of abuse and the recreation of roles within a family. The narcissist wants to live in a family life and fantasy world where there is nothing healthy of nature existing- only chaos and dysfunction. The narcissist will often recreate their family life in a manner to similar to which they were raised.

Within a dysfunctional family unit, the unhealthy, toxic, and often selfish parent or caregiver splits their moral self-image and inferior self-image into two distinct parts and projects it onto their children. As a result, one child becomes the golden child who can do no wrong, while the other becomes the scapegoat. The golden child is the glorified creation of perfection who can do no wrong to the narcissist, despite anything they may do. The scapegoat, is the pinata who is thrown all the blame, hatred, projections, internal rage of the narcissist and other family members on.

The roles involved in the family includes the scapegoat, the enabler, the golden child, the narcissist, lost child, and the mascot or clown.

The Scapegoat

The scapegoat will be used as a punching bag for the narcissist, and in turn other family members will be shown and taught indirectly to take their anger out on the scapegoat, and to subject them to injustices, wickedness, and other unfair punishments, without any fear of repercussions. Those within the family dynamics prey upon this learned behavior and will then cause this pattern of abuse to occur towards the scapegoat usually. The scapegoat will have no way of escaping this damnation or illegal punishment against them since they've done no wrong, and will resort to holding this role, often for a a very long period of time and long after childhood as well.

The golden child and other children or family members involved will feel it is normal to mistreat and project upon the scapegoat and will emulate this abuse through a victim's life. They hold no conscience for their behaviors because they are puppets and mimicries of the narcissist. The narcissist has molded and created these people to be exactly what they are, and for them it is normal, and they have no care how the victim feels. They are taught by the narcissist to ignore the wants, needs, and feelings of the scapegoat, and to show them what they are- a punching bag and someone to project at in hostility or take their anger out on.

Narcissistic families use a scapegoat as a way to protect their egos, discharge themselves from their own negative emotions and create a villain, in order to pathologize and pin all their blames or aggression on. They in turn end up feeling self-righteous and as if they are powerful heroes for committing these unjust actions.

The scapegoat has no family of defending or protecting themselves. They will be silenced by all parties and denigrated further because the narcissist and their cohorts, which will be the other family members will resort to mob mentality and ganging up on this person.

The scapegoat will be taught by the narcissist through extreme devaluing and abuse that their opinion and their self-worth don't matter and that they have no say and no way to stand up for themselves. If a scapegoat stood up for themselves, it would crumble the very core of the dysfunctional narcissistic family, which has relied on this dynamic of purging on the scapegoat in order to release themselves of their own aggressions, sins and burdens. This is a strong and disturbing delusional belief created by the narcissist in their own confused pathological mind, and a concept they mold the other family members into becoming, acting upon and believing as well.

The golden child

The golden child is the narcissist's favorite creation- glorified and loved, and usually not touched but favored in excessive ways by the narcissist- they are the pride and joy of the narcissist and the one who most will emulate the narcissistic parent and turn into a replica of them in some way. The narcissist will rarely hurt, denigrate or even scold thegolden child. They are the narcissist's beloved, the narcissist parent's best friend, and the one the narcissist is not only closest to, but the one who will be groomed to be the narcissist's puppet.

The golden child. The golden child is often a monster like the narcissist. The narcissistic parent groomed the golden child or children to be supporters of this disordered monster in the most disturbing of ways. If a victim ever attempts to malign the narcissist or call them out the golden child will defend the predatory narcissist to the end.

The golden child will always defend the pathology of the narcissist and their behaviors, and employ the exact same behaviors and tactics such as minimizing, denying, or projecting them usually onto the scapegoat. The narcissistic parent could commit crimes, and the golden child wouldn't care and would side with the narcissistic parent no matter what. To the golden child, the narcissistic parent does no wrong. They are emblems of perfection.

The parent hasn't hurt the golden child only showed them respect care and love. The golden child is a perfect image and reflection of the narcissist. They are the narcissist in their children's form, and are there to glorify, give adulation, attention, and praise to the narcissist. If you attempt to tell the golden child of the narcissist's evil or errors, they will often lash out and throw a fit, and refuse to believe, or accept any of this and resort to immediately defending the narcissist, giving defending their behavior, minimizing it, denying it and throw the blame back on the victim just like the narcissist.

The golden child and the co parent are huge enablers of the narcissist and will almost always retraumatize the victim. The golden child will emulate the narcissistic parent and use the victim as a scapegoat. The narcissistic parent has turned everyone against the victim and made them a scapegoat for everyone.

The Enabler

The narcissist is full of enablers in their life those who refuse to stop the abuser from committing their actions towards the victim. The victim is the one constantly suffering, having all sorts of evil hatred and accusations being dumped on them and worse.

What is an enabler? An enabler is someone who is close to the narcissist who supports them in their illegal and wicked disordered actions, cheers on their dysfunction, and allows them to do these things to their victims, or even helps them out. The enabler can be anyone, though it is usually the narcissist's friends, or family members, or a partner or spouse. Enablers have abusive tendencies themselves, or just simply lack introspection or a real conscience and feel that doing this kind of evil to someone is no big deal and don't have the notion to stop it, but rather will join the narcissist.

An enabler in a narcissistic family dynamic is usually the co-parent or spouse and the golden child or other children. The other parent might not be the primary source of abuse going on within the family, or might even be an abuser themselves within the family in different forms. They often will encourage the narcissist or stand by as the narcissist implements their negative behaviors onto the family. The enabler will resort to shaming, mistreating or abusing the scapegoat as well.

The Lost Child

The lost child is categorized by any child in a narcissistic family dynamic that isn't treated like the golden child or the scapegoat. They often resort to developing other behaviors or resort to developing their own skills and talents in order to escape the harrowing situation that might be going on. The lost child will too, resort to mistreating the scapegoat and often grows up feeling dysfunctional and has their own set of issues. The lost child will often mimic the behaviors and dynamics that go on within the family, and join the dysfunctional family dynamics. The lost child often avoids conflict by keeping a low profile.

The lost child is often the invisible or forgotten child in a narcissistic family dynamic, and one who tries to stay quiet. They often resort to other activities as well such as television, fantasies, daydreaming, or keep themselves busy and are sometimes neglected by the abusive parents. The invisible child may or may not be subjected to emotional abuse or some form of abuse, but it is not like the abuse the scapegoat has to endure.

The lost child may resort to escapism and avoid interpersonal interactions and may repress their emotions, or they may do the total opposite and become overly extroverted and resort to engaging in normal healthy activities in order to escape the role they have. Many lost children will feel as if they have no impact on others or the world.

Many children of narcissists will often be placed in several different roles at once, or take on different roles. They may be the oldest child and end up being a scapegoat and playing a hero role as well due to their position in the family. Many children will resort to behaving in different ways in order to avoid the toxic scenario they are a part of. There are many varying issues that children of narcissists will have after all the abuse they have endured from these kinds of parents. They may experience a distrust of others, have internalized self-hatred, low self-esteem, a distrust of authority figures, and be at risk of developing narcissistic personality disorder themselves. They may have a distorted sense of self and ideations about the world and life, or can develop unhealthy romantic relationships They will often enter into adulthood with a host of problems and unresolved issues that need to be addressed by a professional.

Chapter 11

How To Deal With a Narcissist

How to defend yourself against a narcissist

There is no real way to defend yourself against a narcissist or their attacks, except by leaving the area, room, or getting away. Once a narcissist begins to rage, they usually just don't stop. Once they begin their abusive or devaluation phase, they rarely get better. You can ask them to stop, politely ask them to stop yelling at you or being rude, tell them they need to respect you, but they will refuse to stop. If a narcissist has decided to "rage" against a victim, it is something they will not stop, and you will have to resort to just leaving or asking them to leave.

Often times, if you ask them to stop, they will get worse, and get more aggressive towards you in order to prove they are right and you are wrong, and to do the damage to you they initially intended to do. A narcissist will usually rage at their victim to further demean, bring them down or damage them, their psyche, soul and life, and to purge their inner angry self which they have no way of dealing with.

If a narcissist tries to or gets involved in your life in a negative way, you can resort to minimizing contact but always remembering that nothing they do will be fair or for your best interest or interest. They are callous devious predators and will take victims to court, or do horrible things to them only for the desire or pleasure to exert maximum abuse and damage to a victim and often will deny their actions, never care or take responsibility and do not care how a victim feels about the situation or the trauma or suffering they are enduring.

You'll find narcissists destroying families and lives in the courtroom- either as lawyers, or parents, you'll find them in varying professions as doctors or other professionals, yet many are not able to do damage or destruction as they must keep their professions, so they resort to their narcissistic behaviors towards family or those close to them.

You'll find them everywhere in all areas of life, being the negative monsters they are, resorting to their disturbing tactics without a care or thought, while being nice to their friends or those who are their support system or close to them. Many times, you can't even remove them from your life fully, because even if you escape them they will come back to haunt you through different means such as the court system, verbal or emotional abuse in some form, emotional blackmail, aggression, and they might even be docile or nice for long periods of time fooling you into thinking they won't really abuse you again or do any form of real damage or abuse.

Narcissists get you to trust them and pretend they're your best friend

They will pretend to be your closest friend or get you to trust them in some deeper form, despite being the most wicked of abusers and those who have done the most damage in your life. This is only the unhealthy trauma bond they have formed with you, and in some cases you may even be exhibiting some form of Stockholm syndrome by siding with the narcissist and believing that they are good people or by feeling they won't hurt you or have no harmful intentions towards you, which is the norm way of thinking, that most normal people revert back to so they don't have to think evil thoughts about someone or feel that the person wants to do them harm.

Narcissists do not attack or prey upon other narcissists or those with negative traits or sociopathic tendencies. They are predators and will usually prey upon those who possess traits or qualities that are of genuineness, kindness, goodness, and a nature that is different from this particular kind of disordered person.

However, a narcissist may victimize another narcissist if they are unaware the person is a narcissist and got used to abusing them in some form throughout their life. The person may have developed into a narcissist and the abuser has no clue of this and will continue this abuse towards them. A narcissist cannot handle any form of narcissistic abuse towards them in any way, shape or form and will usually internalize it in very unsuccessful ways or externalize it by raging on their victims or lashing out at them.

Learn how to take your energy and life back

Taking care of yourself is important, however it is not what will heal a victim of this nature of abuse. A victim must empower themselves by gaining the right form of therapy and healing, and finding effective strategies of learning how to cope with their situation and learning ways they can break free of this toxic psychopath and especially break the bonds of abuse between the victim and the abuser.

The victim must learn how to gain their energy and power back from the abuser, because really the abuser has stolen most of their energy and soul and will continue this pattern and cycle as long as everyone allows them to, and no one will ever stop them. Even if a narcissist has stopped the major cycle of abuse and seems to be nice for a long period of time, they will almost always revert back to their abusive destructive ways and often it will be extreme in nature and too difficult for the victim to manage.

The narcissist has stolen a victim's life from them- there is no other way to put it. The victim was once a happy, thriving, optimistic, strong person and they have now turned into scared, repressed, disordered people themselves with a host of negative energies, feelings, emotions, issues present.

A narcissist victim's life is a lot like a horror movie. They have been terrorized to extremes in all kinds of ways and need to gain the empowerment necessary to take their life, spirit, soul, and energy back from this frightening monster. If they have escaped the grips of the narcissist, they often still need to heal themselves from the terror they were put through by this person.

Realize they are not your friend, they are your worst enemy

Despite the abuse, or during periods of them behaving normally or even love bombing periods, they will have you fooled into feeling there is some kind of bond between the two of you and it feels very normal to you.

You also may not feel this level of comfort with others, only them. This is a dangerous tactic they use to manipulate you into feeling they are your ally or friend, and worse, this dysfunctional dynamic is what makes up the trauma bonds between you and this predator. They are not someone you should feel comfortable with at all, because you as a confused victim will usually stay this way- distraught and confused due to the nature and amount of abuse that has been done to you.

It's not your fault- any normal person would feel this way. You are a normal healthy person who has been abused in terrifying ways by this predator, and once they are nice to you, then most of the time you are either too frightened to deal with the situation, or feel a level of comfort with them or just ignore the prior abuse that happened because you enjoy peace and do not like conflict the way they do, and just want everything to be ok and peaceful.

You also don't have the energy to fight them any longer, have no idea how to process this situation happening which is too complex to be able to grasp, and lack the internal processes to grasp this level of abnormality that they are.

They are not close to you- they are a predator similar to a sociopath or psychopath out there. Your best interest is not within their realm of intent no matter how nice they seem, or how much they have helped you out. Their only intent is to prey on you in some form, and all the help or nice things they do for you aren't really for you, it's usually for them or for some underlying motive they hold.

Make them fear you in some way and they might behave:

The narcissist has no fear of repercussions which is why they treat the victim the way they do. They've been enabled by almost everyone around them or ignored for their behaviors, and if there is a fear factor involved then they may stop their mistreatment of you. No one has stopped this abuser, and a victim will rarely find people who will be supportive or advocates for the victim.

There are no consequences, repercussions, or fear of any backlash if they do any kind of harm to the victim. If they feared the situation, then they might think twice about how they treat a victim. Try to find a friend or family member who will be your ally and someone who will be your defender, and show the narcissist you're not alone.

Find a way to make them fear you or the situation and getting caught.

Never be alone with a narcissist- narcissists often target those who are alone

Never be alone with a narcissist. If you do not want to be mistreated by a narcissist, have a third party around if they are around. The narcissist will usually target you if they feel they can isolate you effectively through their well thought-out or planned abuse tactics. If there is another abuser or enabler around, they may still resort to their abusive ways, but the narcissist will usually be on their best behavior with others around, and will be kind and nice or act normal. Never be alone with them exclusively. This is a green light for them to behave in any way they want.

Don't react- walk away

Victims usually argue and fight with a narcissist because it's the normal thing to do. They are impervious to the narcissist's true intent, which is to get reactions out of a victim, which is narcissistic supply to their sickness, evil, and disordered self and behavior. They are extremely angry inside and seek to generate these arguments and reactions from their victim. It not only makes them feel validated in some form, it's their way of purging their internal anger and hatred onto the victim and making the victim feel their pain, and then forcing the victim to turn into them by being angry and lashing out, or arguing back.

Never react to a narcissist, just walk away, or tell them to leave your presence. Most of the time, they will not leave and will stay and become even more hostile. They will do this to prove to the victim they possess no evil in them and anything they do is perfect, and to further traumatize and damage a victim, and make them suffer, and throw more negativity onto them. A narcissist will constantly damage a victim internally. Arguments of this nature are also fun for the narcissist. It feeds their warped need to feel grandiose or powerful.

Don't agree with them or be doting

You don't want to turn into a disordered person like them. If you do want to avoid conflict, you can agree with them for a moment just to get them to leave the situation

and not throw their narcissistic anger and rage on you, but it's important to stay true to your beliefs, morals and integrity. They have none of these qualities or characteristics and don't care how they behave or about their immoral actions.

Believe in yourself, your thoughts and reactions

You are the sane normal one, they are sick disordered person with a mental illness. You are not the crazy disordered one as they project onto you or try to make you out to be, you're normal, they're not. Trust yourself and your instincts, and never trust them.

Get someone else to be with you- never be alone with them, they use that as an opportunity to mistreat or abuse you. You always want someone else to be around because they will cause the narcissist to behave themselves in some form most of the time.

You are never safe with a narcissist

You are never safe around them. They are not the safe close person they have groomed you into thinking they are. You might think they are a close friend or family member, but they are never around you to be of your best interest. Their interest is mostly to harm you in some form, even if they are acting or seem nice at the time. They are disordered predators, and you need to treat them as such. Never feel safe or comfortable around them, they most likely have ruined your life, and yet are still somehow in your life because you were unable to discard them or get away from them.

Never trust them or their intentions

Never trust their actions, words, or behaviors because they rarely have good intentions. Their goal for their targets or victims is extreme pain and trauma and not much else. They seek to destroy people's lives, not just do abuse on the surface. They shatter and ruin lives, people's minds, souls, their goal is to ruin everything for a person. They are not normal, kind, healthy people like they portray themselves to be. They will only have the most ill intentions for someone.

Cut off contact with them

Cut off any form of contact with them- you have no choice. You can't associate yourself with this person in any form. Their goal for a victim is only something very drastically negative or evil in nature, and they are of no benefit to a person. Most narcissists are just toxic predators, and need to be removed from a person's life in some way. Discard them for all the evil, terrible things they have done to you.

Find a mediator or third party who can help deal with the situation

This might be really difficult, but finding a mediator or third party who can talk to the narcissist in some form or mediate between the victim and predator can be some way of dealing with their brutal behavior and actions. It's difficult for this to work, because the narcissist or abuser will usually employ tactics such as denying the abuse, gaslighting, making the victim out to be abusive or crazy, but it's a chance to attempt to get some assistance in dealing with a very difficult negative situation.

Never doubt your own perceptions or confidence

You are the sane, normal amazing person. They are not. Narcissists will gaslight a victim, blame them for anything, and deny any abuse ever happened. They will seriously mess with a person's mind and psyche in huge ways. They want a target to doubt their own selves, beliefs, ideas, and turn into a disordered shell of hate and confusion just like they are. It's important to never doubt your own beliefs or perceptions and to stay true to yourself, your confidence and your wonderful nature. You are normal, they are not.

Narcissists will rarely heal or ever change

An abuser, especially a narcissist will ever heal or change their behaviors, attitudes and actions towards the victim or the situation going on. They will never come to realizations of their abusive actions or how it affects the victim, and will just continue to show no remorse for their behaviors or how a victim feels. Narcissists might apologize sometimes or pretend to be apologetic or say they didn't mean it, but their apologies are all fake. They will usually resort to their abusive actions or behaviors consciously or unconsciously, and might even employ them in a harsher manner towards a target, after a false apology.

Their behaviors towards a victim have become ingrained in them, and they will never truly reflect inwards, or analyze any of their thoughts or actions, only implement them in more disturbing ways and patterns. They are unable to heal because of the nature of their disorder and the level of dysfunction they possess. They are just that sick and mentally ill, they will never come to realization of their actions, and in turn will usually not be able to heal from their sickness. Even if they did, internally they are unable to heal, and their natures and inner selves are just too damaged.

Chapter 12

How To Empower Yourself Against a Narcissist

Have a plan of action to take:

Have a plan of action you want to take. It's extremely important that you have a plan of action that you want to create for yourself in order to break free of the abuser, and so you can heal for yourself.

This is extremely important for you as the victim for the victim is usually caught in the clutches of a darkness and scenario that is life-threatening life altering and one that may have already done immense damage to their lives and to their selves. You can't just get help by reading books and stories of others with the hopes of getting away, healing, or recovering from this kind of abuse.

You must have a plan of action you want to take and have a support system in some form that will help out with carrying out this plan. You may be able to do it on your own as well and this is necessary. You need extreme amounts of support, self-care, and a modality of therapy that will help to heal your trauma and your childhood most likely or anything that was present that might be contributing or connected to what might be happening in your present situation.

As a victim of abuse, you are in extreme need of deep and important healing, inner development and cultivation, and ways of being able to handle the abuse being done and how to gain your strength and power back and to be able to get away from the abuser and break ties. Breaking ties in a healthy way is very important and it's important to just diminish contact with them altogether.

You have deep seated trauma and emotional wounds that need to be healed and taken care of and addressed. Your feelings matter, and it's a difficult process to endure and have to even begin because you will have to address all the abuse that has been done to you, with attempts of regaining and recovering your own true self- the healthy you you once were as opposed to the damaged scared victim this perpetrator has made you.

Having a strong support system is the number one plan of action you may want to take which is finding a number of supporters and helpers who can aid and assist you with the things you have been through and who can support you in any form through this process. You also need someone or people who can be guides aiding and helping you out during this difficult time in your life.

Most of the time, the victim just wants things to be back to normal with the narcissist. They wish and desire they could maintain a peaceful reality with them, but this is something that can't be done in a normal way- the narcissist will always go back to their abusive ways at some point and the devaluation phase will begin.

Get away from them, cut off contact, sever all ties

The only way to empower yourself against a narcissist is to get away from them, cut off all or most contact or have very minimal contact with them. Never perceive them as a true friend, lover, savior, family member relative or anyone there to help you no matter how much good they have done for you. They aren't your friend or lover or someone who cares about you.

They are someone there to destroy you and cause you great harm and often, they will have done many nice things for you confusing you into thinking they care for you or have good intent for you, which isn't the case. This is part of the manipulation they do to those they victimize or target. They fool you into thinking they are your friend, family member or just someone who is a normal nice friend to you, and may often shower you with gifts, or have some form of financial dominance over you.

They may give you nice things or have been 'nice' for a longer period of time, so you forget about all the abuse they have done to you. Often they might be nice but then throw some abusive behaviors in there intermittently, to keep you down or steal your energy, and that's so they can make sure you never regain your true strength or true nature again- so you'll be down in the dumps, unsure of yourself, lacking true confidence, and never regain your true spirit and will always be victimized by other abusers or low energy mean, negative people.

It's often claimed that narcissists or abusers of their nature sprinkle people with positivity and positive reinforcement or gifts in the midst of their abuse, which is very true as well, but they also might be "nice" or behave normally for periods of time and jump in with abusive behaviors and tactics just to further destabilize a victim's internal self and sense of self-worth. They want to keep reminding the victim of who they are now, and who the narcissist wants them to be- the narcissist's punching bag, and the narcissist is a often a machine of rage.

It's important to cut off all contact with them- try to block them if you can from all social media, or minimize contact as much as possible if you feel you can't right away. Narcissists often times will have created the false perception that they are very close to you in some form, or that you feel comfortable talking to them almost like a family member, or they might be a family member who you have grown to feel a certain level of comfort with.

Find a support group or healthy people or friends:

Find or create a group or supportive people who aren't narcissists or figure out how to find good friends even one or two who are healthy and will be there for you in your best interest, who can be your allies, and take the place of this scary predator, rather than allowing the narcissist to make you believe the false pretense that they are your friend or supporter or there for you as any form of support.

You need a support system and an army of this nature to be with you and by your side, so that the narcissist can have less power and dominance over you. Once you have a healthy support system, the narcissist will have less of an effect on you, and you'll have more positive interactions and people in your life to turn to, rather than this predator.

This will make the presence of this predator in your life much less, and they will soon dwindle into the nothingness they are in your reality. The narcissist needs to be nothing in your world and reality. They are not someone important- they are a dangerous dark predator and you must comprehend this. Most narcissists are extremely weak, fragile and broken inside. They are not strong, powerful people just disordered miscreants.

Find a therapist to get necessary healing and therapy

Finding a therapist to heal from all of the trauma and negative emotions and damage the narcissist has done to your life is extremely important. It's very important for a victim of narcissistic abuse, or any form of abuse to find a licensed therapist who can help them understand their situation, deal with it and heal from it. It's very difficult for narcissistic abuse victims to find therapists because often they have tried at some point and therapy either didn't work for them, or they may have encountered bad therapists or people who may have been narcissistic in nature themselves.

The nature of narcissistic abuse is becoming more well-known today, but years ago and even now there are many therapists who are not equipped with the knowledge of how to handle those who have been abused or victimized, or in plain terms there are therapists who really don't want to help others, and may take advantage of those who were abused or victimized by using it against them.

This is a common thing many victims of abuse have dealt with in therapy and it's not always easy to find a decent therapist who is good for the victim. The victim needs empowerment, enlightenment about narcissism and abuse, ideas on how to cope with the abuse, techniques for dealing with the abuse, ways of getting support and healing, and ways of meeting new people and finding new friends.

Therapy is extremely important because of the nature of abuse being done and the necessity to heal any trauma energies present.

Empower Yourself- Learn How to take your life and power back

It's important to implement any form of self-care or taking care of oneself. You must focus on having different forms of healthy narcissism which is self-love and understanding that you are not the problem, weak, an easy target etc. There is nothing wrong with you. You are very normal, and even if you're not totally normal, that's ok- you're not abnormal or like them. The narcissist's victims are most likely extremely talented, bright indiviudals who are very intelligent and have great qualities about them.

This is why the narcissistic disordered abuser chose these people to target, because they could gain the most from breaking them down or destroying their lives in some form. Many times, the narcissists are also even more attached to these people, and they fear their progression, or they fear their own loneliness and the victim getting away from them. The narcissist is the disordered damaged individual who is similar to a sociopath in nature. They are not normal and are the ones in desperate need of mental help and therapy.

Focus on yourself, and how important your healing is, and for you to regain yourself back to the person you used to be- a happy, healthy, thriving individual with goals in life, or just true happiness. That was before the narcissist came into the picture to ruin you in ways you can't describe.

Listen to positive affirmations

It's important to love yourself, and have any form of confidence or happiness you can, and to continuously remind yourself that you are a worthy valid important person. Positive affirmations can help with regaining and helping to rebuild your self-esteem in some form and to reprogram your mind with positive thoughts, rather than the negativity the narcissist has thrown into you.

Begin to journal your situation

Write about your situation- it may be difficult but begin to write about your situation or the experiences you are encountering. Though it may be difficult with narcissistic abuse because of the amount of abusive tactics that are used against a victim and the shock and trauma they are usually in.

Writing about your experiences can help validate them and remind you that they are real and that your feelings are real, though a victim doesn't necessarily want to relive the abuse through writing and want to be reminded of it daily. Studies have shown that there are tremendous benefits that come with journaling and writing down a person's situation. Begin to write about your stories and situations, and then think about ways you can rewrite the story or change it within your life. Focus on the positive aspects in your life and begin building on them.

Use your situation to write about your experiences and to help others

You can often write about your experiences with a narcissist and use that to help others going through the same thing. You can turn the situation the narcissist did to you as ammunition to use against them, to help other people being victimized unfairly and to help empower them. Narcissists and abusers don't want you to progress or succeed, or gain strength and other abusers don't want their victims to gain any form of strength either or to move on from them.

You have the ability to actually empower other victims and others in the situation you're having to endure. Many times, people are put through certain scenarios in life, so they can actually turn around and use it to help others. You have the ability to take your negative experiences with a narcissist or abuser, and help others gain huge advances in their own life, escape an abuser, and find methods to gain their strength and life back. You can change and help people's lives.

Search online for forums on narcissism and other survivor's experiences

It's helpful to search online for forums about narcissism, such as platforms like reddit, which have groups that are designed specifically for victims who are dealing with narcissistic abuse. The internet isn't always the best place for survivors of abuse to be in only because it's an open forum and anyone can write what they want, but it can be helpful to know that you're not alone- that there are many others with stories and situations just like yourself, and you may get helpful advice from others on how to deal with the abuse you are going through.

It can also be comforting in some sense knowing you're not alone and there are others going through the same situation you are, though it usually doesn't help the situation but reading about how other people might cope with the situation can effectively have a positive impact on you.

Talk to friends or family members if you're able to

Talk to anyone you can who is there to help you and help your growth. Find friends or family members you can go to for any form of support. It's difficult for people to find support because victims usually feel ashamed and terrified of going to others attempting to get help, and maybe they have tried and have been shunned in some form or haven't received the responses they wanted or expected. Often times, abuse victims are surrounded by dangerous, pathological people and feel they have no positive support system or anyone to turn to.

Finding a support system of this nature might be difficult, but it's extremely important that the narcissist is not one of the few forms of support you have in life or one of your few supporters or friends. You can never feel safe with a narcissist, for they are not there for your best interest and will always lash back out at you or target you in some way.

Call hotlines if you're in need of immediate support or therapy. There are many abuse and crisis hotlines with supportive people and counselors there ready to talk to you about your situation. There is also a national domestic violent hotline which is very helpful in helping people with different forms of partner abuse.

Learn effective ways of coping with mistreatment or abuse
This is your life and they don't belong in it

Learn effective ways of dealing with mistreatment or abuse and ways you can better and empower yourself and not allow the narcissist or abuser to do any form of harm to you. You are too good for the narcissist- you are above them and better than them. They do not deserve to be anywhere near you or around you.

Never allow them the place to do any form or harm towards you in your life. This is 'your' life, not theirs. If they aren't benefiting you in some way, then you need to cut ties with them. You do not need them in any way- this is a myth they have not only created in your mind, but it has become very an abnormal feeling that has become ingrained, and it is also untrue.

You do not need the narcissist, they are the ones that are empty and void of feelings and a life, they need you. The concept of needing the narcissist is also an illogical and abnormal way of thinking that this disordered creature has placed in your psyche, soul and body through extreme terror and trauma-based fear. Why would you need someone who abuses you in any way? You may feel you need them for many reasons but really you don't. They also do not belong anywhere near you or in your life. It's your life and it's your choice who you want in it.

Try to go to group therapy with the narcissist so maybe they can be exposed and might minimize their mistreatment of you

It's very difficult to go to therapy with a narcissist because most of the time, they will not go or admit they are doing anything wrong to you. They are in deep denial of everything they have done and it's also exposing you to this predator in a deeper more painful way, which might be difficult for a victim to handle.

However, going to therapy could result in the narcissist being exposed, gaining some form of realization within themselves that they could treat you differently, or out of fear of being exposed in various forms and even to their own selves, they may try to change their attitude towards you.

Therapy could also be dangerous for the victim, because the narcissist might have some form of a narcissistic or psychotic break, or be unable to handle what is being said about them, thought of them or they themselves being unable to realize the truth or internalize any of it normally. They may further lash out or become even more abusive.

Set goals for the therapy you plan to do

Therapy is one of the most important ways a victim will effectively heal and learn how to handle the toxic negativity they have been through. A victim must focus on finding a reputable and helpful therapist who they can confide in, trust, and who is trained in dealing with this specific kind of abuse. Set realistic goals for the kind of therapy you want to do, and what you plan to gain from it.

Set life goals you have and begin to implement them:

The narcissist will try to stop you from achieving your life goals, or any life goal. Sometimes, they won't care but if you are taking a huge step to benefit yourself, your success or get away from them or their abuse, they will jump in to stop you. The narcissist doesn't want you to be happy, to shine, to succeed, to do great things, to achieve your life's goal or purpose, or to live in peace and harmony. They want you to suffer- and not much else. You are a tool and object to this confused clueless person and they only want you to be in a constant state of suffering, or in a place of destruction.

You must make your goals in life manifest, for the narcissist will only be there to make sure this doesn't happen. You are deserving of good things in life- not some disordered creature to ruin you. You are not a punching bag for some mentally ill psychopath that has nothing better to do with their life or time.

The narcissist stole your very life, soul, and spirit from you in some form and it's important to get back to the person you were before the narcissist invaded your life. Did you have any goals in life? Were there important things you planned on doing and now all you can think about is the abuse? Most victims are very broken and in desperate need of healing and therapy, but they are able to set important goals for themselves and their life and begin to implement them slowly.

Begin to set goals for yourself. What kind of goals do you have or did you have in life, that were somehow thwarted by the narcissist?

Get a new job, try to find a better position in the career field you're in, go back to school and get a higher degree, volunteer somewhere, set new goals in life. Did you have important things you planned on doing in life before this negative person came into it? You do have the power to set life goals and begin to make them happen and come into existence.

Learn about narcissists and how other survivors healed

It always helps to learn about narcissists and their disorder, and to read or listen to books of other survivor's experiences or coping mechanisms, and techniques they've used to heal from being victim's of this person, and ways they were able to deal with their situation. You'll find hundreds of survivors and people out there who have written about their experiences and who have effective ways of dealing with these narcissists.

It's important not just to read and learn about narcissism and this disorder, but to get therapy, heal in any form possible, and to talk to experts or supportive people who can better you or your life and who are there to assist you in making changes or helping you gain the strength to break ties with this abuser.

You matter and you are an extremely important individual, not a punching bag for a narcissist and an abuser. Often times, victims are dealing with multiple narcissists at once or various forms of narcissists and abusers and it's a very difficult and challenging scenario to be a part of. The victim starts to feel as if they are nothing, or just a powerless, abused nobody who can't fight or handle these disordered people. It's very difficult to face this kind of reality or abuse situation.

Feeling empowered or even a worthy valid human can be incredibly hard. People in this dangerous situation need to figure out how to cut ties with these abusers in their life and to get help fast. The damage done by multiple narcissists at once cannot be described in words. Often times, people find themselves sandwiched in between these abusers going from one abusive person to the next. They are often surrounded by toxic people of this nature.

Protect yourself and your boundaries

You have been devalued, abused, and the attacker has destroyed your self-worth and boundaries. You lived a healthy, happy life prior to the narcissist's unwarranted invasion, and things are not going to get back to the way you want them to be until you remove this person from your life. Protect yourself and your boundaries. You are deserving of only love, healing, positive attention, and positive, caring loving people. You are not deserving of the abuse the narcissist is doing to you.

Find effective ways of strengthening your boundaries, and creating healthy bonds with healthy people, and run from the disordered creature that is just doing so much dangerous abuse to you and creating trauma bonds. Learn ways to strengthen your boundaries and learn to gain your self-worth and esteem back so you can create the healthy boundaries you once had.

I am strong

I am worthy

I deserve to be loved and treated with respect

I deserve only loving caring relationships

I believe in myself

I matter, my feelings matter

I am important and worthy

My feelings and thoughts are important

I am very intelligent

I am independent and a hard worker

Live for yourself, not for the narcissist

It's a difficult concept to comprehend, but you are living for this disordered abuser who has ruined your life. You are not living for yourself. You are not in need of the narcissist, that feeling of dependency is often the narcissist projecting their emotions onto you emotionally or through energy unconsciously, or consciously, and through their abusive behaviors.

You need to start living for yourself, and focusing on yourself exclusively. Your feelings, needs and wants matter, not the narcissist, their cohorts, other family members, enablers, or friends. They are living their lives happily usually and successfully in some form, while they have created this dysfunction of taking their anger out on you, mocking you, degrading you in some way or just ruining you or your life. You need to focus on living for what is best for you, and implement this concept in your daily life. Never allow them to hurt you or take control of your life or emotions.

The narcissist usually needs the victim, and no one would want some disordered abuser needing them or anywhere in their life. The victim often feels a false sense of being unable to severe the bond between they and the abuser. That's because of all the negative interactions that have occurred, trauma bonds, and very negative energy that the abuser has thrown upon the narcissist.

Your energy and soul is full of this toxic person's energy and it's very damaging and painful. The narcissist has stolen most of your power, which is your energy and soul and thrown their own disordered negative dark energy into you, and formed a dysfunctional bond right there which is why you feel you can't get away from the narcissist or abuser.

The trauma bond is energetic in nature, as well as emotional. Since the narcissist has stolen most of your energy and power and holds it within them, and raged so much evil and hate upon you, you feel weak and powerless. This is why a victim feels unable to get away from the abuser, and feels they have some kind of upper hand or strength over them. The narcissist has no real power over you- they are weak, disordered, inferior people who shouldn't be anywhere near a victim.

Live for yourself- it's your life and you matter. They shouldn't be anywhere near you or in your amazing life where you deserve to create and have positive and loving experiences, not the negativity and hatred they are full of. They are full of negativity and hatred and without you will self-destruct in some way. They may survive their mental illness and disorder and seem as if they are doing ok, but they are destroying themselves within. They will never be truly happy, and they don't deserve to be anywhere near someone like you. You are far above them. Stop living for the narcissist or allowing them to take your power and energy, or giving them any part of your love, gifts or presence.

It's my life, not the narcissist's life

I don't want them in my life anymore- they don't belong in it

my life matters- I need to create loving healthy bonds and relationships

I can interact with others- there is nothing wrong with me

There is something very wrong with the narcissist or the abuser

It's not my fault they mistreated or abused me, it's their fault

I am not guilty of what the abuser has done to me or to others

Discard the Narcissist

It's important to discard the narcissist and remove them from your life. They have created extreme dysfunction inside of you and in your life. They do not belong in your life in any way or form. Contrary to what someone thinks, the victim has the upper hand. They have the ability and power to discard the narcissist and remove this toxic predator and sociopath from their life. They are a destructive predator that seeks to only wreak havoc in your life, and not much else.

> I do not need this person
>
> the narcissist doesn't belong in my life
>
> I deserve better than this toxic person
>
> This abuser doesn't deserve to be anywhere near me
>
> I deserve only love and healthy loving relationships
>
> I can easily remove this person from my life
>
> This person does not belong in my life or anywhere near me
>
> I deserve to only be cherished and loved

Chapter 13

Ways to Heal From Narcissistic Abuse

You must somehow take your power back from the narcissist, after all they have stolen most of your energy, life force and soul from you. This is not easy to do. Even if you have recovered or healed and gained your power or strength back in some form, they might be around to destroy you and take it again, or will revert to their abusive ways if they get a chance to be around you.

Healing from the abuse and trauma done to you comes with the understanding that you need to comprehend the concepts of what they have done to you, and find effective ways of handling it, and removing yourself from the situation, removing that person's influence in your life, and understanding the concept of your place within the scenario of abuse. Abuse comes with power and control, and it is not really about the victim, but about how the abuser feels internally and within their own selves.

The narcissist doesn't hate you (they might be envious of you), they aren't targeting you because you're weak or traumatized or different, or something is wrong with you. The narcissist is a predator, and this predator had an opportunity or a situation where they either needed to begin abusing someone, or just chose to do it for other reasons.

They are a dangerous person for you, and not beneficial to you in any way. You need to heal from their abuse and remove them from your life or minimize contact in some way. Don't allow the narcissist to be primary in your life, because they usually are with their victims. Bring others into your life, so the narcissist is simply just out of your life, or someone who has no significance in your life or to you.

Immerse yourself and your soul in positive fun activities

You must immerse yourself with positive, uplifting, energetically helping and healing activities as possible.

I live in Florida and often went to Disney world to heal from all the trauma and abuse that I had endured as a victim of narcissistic mistreatment. I found that the atmosphere in these locations is usually full of fun spirited positive and healing energy, and everyone is there to have a great time and have fun. There are children everywhere and people are in a good mood. Negative people might say that theme parks are hot, full of kids, crowded, tiring but positive people wanting to heal will perceive the flip side of this.

At first, I thought it was a silly way of attempting to heal from the experiences I had been through, but it was actually very beneficial in some form. Now therapy and support is the most important aspect of a person's healing, but engulfing yourself in positive, fun experiences will help as well, and in turn bring positivity to your life, and allow you to heal in many ways. Repeat doing these positive things for yourself, and you'll find that you're on a pathway to actually healing and helping yourself, strengthening your positive energy, and becoming empowered.

It is extremely important for a victim of any kind of abuse to immerse themselves in fun, amazing, positive activities that will only be of benefit to them and these experiences will in turn heal them in a huge way and allow the healing within to continue to occur. Abuse victims are often full of traumatic energy that is full of chaos and is in deep need of healing, uplifting, love and positivity of many kinds.

- heal the trauma energy
- do as many positive uplifting things as you can
- do fun, positive things that give your soul and spirit the love, healing and
- energy that it deserves.

This doesn't often involve taking yourself out to dinner, but if that is positive for you then definitely do it. Most victims of abuse are not strong enough to do out to dinner alone, they lack the energetic, mental strength or self-esteem to be able to do it or cope with it.

- do anything positive for yourself- go to theme parks, ride fun cute rides, do things that uplift and bring joy and goodness to the soul and to your spirit, that cleanse and bring your energy up and rid you of the negative energy and evil that is the narcissist.
- It's extremely important to immerse yourself in as many healing, fun activities as you can.

- Go to theme parks- their atmosphere is full of fun positive uplifting energy, and various rides are interesting fun ways of healing the soul and mind
- Go to a religious speaking event, go to a local festival or bazaar. Go shopping at a fun cute store.
- Go to a movie, play mini golf, take up a sport or activity. Movies are a relaxing way of re-energizing one's self, and allowing them to become immersed in something else, and is full of good energy
- Join meetup groups and meet like-minded people who enjoy going out to restaurants, or learning new things.
- Take up a new hobby.
- Go back to school, or take a class at a local university.
- Go sing karaoke. Maybe you had dreams of becoming a singer, or had aspirations to be a lawyer. Maybe you just wanted to get a job at a local store.
- Go to a therapist, to find and receive support in some form
- Use therapy to help you heal and remove and destroy trauma bonds, or any kind of negativity that has ensued in the situation between you and the abuser
- Buy plants for yourself, or to place in your home
- Decorate your home with positive, uplifting objects

- go to group therapy if you can find it to get support from peers, and people around you experiencing similar situations.
- Find healing through different modalities such as spirituality, reiki, energy healing, or learning about these concepts
- Become a teacher and speaker and tell others your story or situation. Use your story and situation to help and empower others. Everyone can learn from other people's life experiences. Teaching others or speaking can be very empowering and allow you to feel you have a sense of purpose or a great achievement you are pursuing and allow you to influence many people's lives or other people's lives
- Go to the gym and workout, work on yourself and your body
- Go to the beach, on a boat- water can be very healing a soothing for a person's life and soul. Salt water is especially beneficial to others, and even helps remove negative energies from a person.
- Take a cruise or a vacation- you definitely deserve it. Find a way to do it and use your experiences to gain amazing new insight, experiences, fun, and newfound energy into your body and soul

- Get a massage- you definitely need one. Your internal makeup is full of all kinds of pent up tension and negative emotions. It can help release negative energies and allow the body to heal
- Get acupuncture done. Find a spiritual healer or someone who can help you heal internally, spiritually and energetically, and someone who can help you remove negative energies or bonds that might be there.
- Reinforce positive beliefs in your mind and spirit using positive affirmations

Therapy and getting support is often the best and primary form of healing. It's extremely important to do your diligence in finding a safe, helpful therapist who can guide you into healing all the trauma and abuse that has been done, and filling it with love, light and positive energy. Your subconscious mind also has to be filled with positive thoughts, and you need a plan of action to take to cut ties with the abuser and toxic person in your life, or minimize contact, no matter how difficult it may seem.

I am safe

I am healed

My life is full of beautiful abundance, joy, and positivity

I am surrounded by a supportive and kind network of people

I have people I know who are safe and healthy to be around

I refuse to be around any kind of toxic people or people who are negative to me

Write a list of positive things about yourself

Think of 50 positive things about yourself, and begin to write them down and journal them. Remind yourself everyday of all of these amazing qualities that you possess and know that you are a great, wonderful person who isn't a punching bag for an abuser. Your feelings matter and you are worthy and important.

Make your life goals manifest
Know that they are not living happy normal lives

They are usually living in misery and darkness. They are not living happy normal lives- they live in a state of darkness and evil.

Always know that there is hope and good for you in life

You are deserving of only respect and the best treatment- not some disordered monster to destroy you and do abuse and destruction that is too shocking to comprehend.

Surround yourself with positive people

You need to surround yourself with people who will cheer you on, benefit you, be positive and strong good influences in your life. You need a strong support system of positive good healthy decent people and people Like yourself, not toxic painful people who choose to terrorize you

You need to be around benevolent positive good people, not people who are similar to the narcissist. You are not negative like them, you are full of positivity and goodness. You have to find people who love and appreciate who you are, and who are honored to be around you or in your presence, and who will respect you, and treat you with kindness, and with the respect and care you deserved to be treated with only.

Just remember. Narcissists or abusers can't or won't appreciate all the great things you bring or possess. They refuse to, will not or don't have the capability to appreciate you for you and you are amazing! You have to find someone who appreciates you for being yourself, and since you're so great and wonderful they simply can't.

They are full of envy and jealousy and may try to bring you down rather than resonate with your positivity. And it's because they usually can't since deep within they are full of anger toxicity hatred lack empathy and are full of negativity.

You deserve to be happy and successful just like they are. You don't deserve to be torn down, mistreated, destroyed or abused in any form.

The narcissist doesn't want you to heal- they don't want you to progress. They don't want you to be your very all or do all of the amazing things that you had planned to do. They want you to suffer, remain destroyed, never recover, heal or get any form of help. They want these dangerous painful interactions and dynamics to occur for a long time, permanently, or for as long as the narcissist wants.

Love yourself, and those who love you, not the narcissist

You must love yourself, and not the narcissist, for the narcissist does not love you. It may be a partner, spouse, parent, child, friend, co-worker. It doesn't matter who the narcissist is, but they simply do not love or care for you at all. This is why they are stealing your positive energy and power and giving it away to others, while weakening and destroying you in ways you can't imagine. They don't care about you and you are just an object for them, though it's hard to imagine sometimes.

Somewhere deep down you think that person may care for you in some form, but really they don't and why would you want them to care for you anyway. They are sick, destructive, dark evil creatures, despite the show they put on for others. You have to accept the fact that they really don't care about the person they victimized, but more importantly, that you need to just remove them from your life in any way, and stop loving them because they are toxic for you, or dangerous and do not feel the same way back, or love you in any way or a healthy way.

Protect yourself, your life and your space

It's your life and your space, you should never allow abusers or people who mistreat or abuse you into it- you can live and do without them, you just feel you can't because they have destroyed your psyche and many parts to you and hurt your soul and damaged you in many ways, and you feel you cant move on on your own or feel too weak. You are an amazing person and deserve only the best and more. You are a caring, kind person and more than that.

You wouldn't allow a dangerous stranger into your life- you'd get rid of them fast, so why allow the narcissist in your life or let them do these evil things to you just because they were someone who seemed close to you. They are not close to you, they are simply there to hurt, destroy or damage you. Even if they help you in some way, it doesn't mean you keep ties with them you need to focus on removing them from your life.

Practice extreme self-care.

Yes self-care is very important- it's important to understand that you are valuable and important and so is your time or life. Abusers often make you feel as if you don't matter or you are unworthy or just deserving of abuse, and it's hard to convince yourself otherwise. You are deserving only of respect and love.

Love yourself first and foremost, even if you don't want to because you'd rather love others first which is how most people tend to feel. It's important to love yourself and care for your wants and needs. Take care of yourself and your body. Eat nourishing healthy foods that will make you feel good about yourself. Go to a gym and workout- take care of your body. Don't neglect yourself, your needs or feelings because you are being abused or your life is being ruined by an abuser or predator. Focus on the fact that your opinion matters, and your voice matters.

Replace negative thoughts, behaviors, and patterns with positive ones

Everytime a negative thought arises, replace it with a positive one. If you're feeling a negative idea or concept about your life or the abuser, recreate the story and create a positive one. Shift your thinking and focus on the positive aspects in your life, and let the negative ones get drowned out. Don't think of the abusive person as powerful or above you. Try not to hold too much aggression or fear about the situation. Think of all the great positive things in your life, and shift your focus to extremely positive, beneficial thoughts, and eliminate any negative thinking or focus on the abuser that you have.

Good things are happening in my life

I love myself unconditionally

I am a beautiful, wonderful and blessed person

I am full of an abundance of blessings and joy

Good people come into my life everyday

I am surrounded by an amazing support system

I love to be around myself

Hopefully this book gave you some insight into the nature of narcissism, and narcissistic abuse and gave you some coping mechanisms and techniques that will enable you to gain power over anyone trying to harm or manipulate you or someone you know. No one, especially good decent people, deserves the wrath or abuse of the narcissist and there are effective ways and methods of getting away and breaking ties with these kinds of people.

You may feel as if there is no hope, but there is a tremendous amount of hope and many people who have successfully cut ties with an abuser and have moved onto having flourishing and healthy lives.

There are many resources out there that can assist someone with dealing with this nature of abuse.

www.ingramcontent.com/pod-product-compliance
Lightning Source LLC
LaVergne TN
LVHW012014060526
838201LV00061B/4305